E. M.
Bounds

WOMEN OF FAITH SERIES

Amy Carmichael
Corrie ten Boom
Florence Nightingale
Gladys Aylward

Isobel Kuhn
Joni
Mary Slessor

MEN OF FAITH SERIES

Andrew Murray
Borden of Yale
Brother Andrew
C. S. Lewis
Charles Colson
Charles Finney
Charles Spurgeon
D. L. Moody
E. M. Bounds
Eric Liddell
George Muller
Hudson Taylor

Jim Elliot
Jonathan Goforth
John Hyde
John Newton
John Paton
John Wesley
Luis Palau
Martin Luther
Oswald Chambers
Samuel Morris
William Booth
William Carey

WOMEN AND MEN OF FAITH

John and Betty Stam
Francis and Edith Schaeffer

OTHER BIOGRAPHIES FROM BETHANY HOUSE

Autobiography of Charles Finney
George MacDonald: Scotland's Beloved Storyteller
Hannah Whitall Smith
Help Me Remember, Help Me Forget (Robert Sadler)
Janette Oke: A Heart for the Prairie
Miracle in the Mirror (Nita Edwards)
Of Whom the World Was Not Worthy (Jakob Kovac family)

E. M. Bounds

Darrel D. King

BETHANY HOUSE PUBLISHERS
MINNEAPOLIS, MINNESOTA 55438

E. M. Bounds
Copyright © 1998
Darrel D. King

Cover by Dan Thornberg,
Bethany House Publishers staff artist.

Scripture quotations are from the *King James Version* of
the Bible.

Published by Bethany House Publishers
A Ministry of Bethany Fellowship, Inc.
11300 Hampshire Avenue South
Minneapolis, Minnesota 55438

Printed in the United States of America by
Bethany Press International,
Minneapolis, Minnesota 55438

Library of Congress Catalog Number applied for

ISBN 0–7642–2009–8

With special thanks:
For their love, encouragement,
sacrifice, and dedication.
Jan King, my wife, Beth and Sara, my daughters.
To the Bounds family:
With Rosemary Bounds Reynolds,
much thanks and gratitude is extended,
and with her encouragement and permission,
this volume is dedicated to the Bounds family,
and to what God has performed
through Edward McKendree Bounds.
To Rev. M. Calvin Yarbrough, my pastor,
and to the people of Metro Heights Baptist Church,
Stockbridge, Georgia.
To my co-laborer and friend Karen Barrett;
her husband, Kevin; Carrie, her daughter;
Zach, her son.
Without Karen's help, assistance, encouragement,
skill, and gifts, this material would still be
in the form of notes accumulating dust
in a box of reminders and remembrances.
To the many others throughout the years
who have encouraged me and prodded me along
to share this volume, my thanks to them.

DR. DARREL KING is president of the E. M. Bounds School of Prayer in Conyers, Georgia, and holds a D.Min. from Luther Rice Seminary and a ThD., PhD. from Mid-Atlantic. Long active in church and parachurch ministry, he served with World Literature Crusade, leading Change the World Schools of Prayer, and also worked in the office of Prayer and Spiritual Awakening with the North Atlantic Mission Board of the Southern Baptist Convention, serving with YouthLink 2000. He and his wife, Jan, have two daughters and live in Conyers, Georgia.

Contents

Introduction

God, who created the heavens and the earth, has found individuals available, trusting, and obedient, who have been spiritual "shooting stars." Their lives have been bright stars of enlightenment and inspiration for the church.

This book is about one of those individuals. A choice vessel that God used mightily to inform and inspire Christian people to bow before God in prayer. God used Edward McKendree Bounds as His gift to the church in America to call His people back to himself. He used Bounds' writings to call people to become missionaries of prayer so that the world might see the Gospel of Christ, His power, and glory.

Even since the death of E. M. Bounds, his books have impacted pastor after pastor, churchman after churchman, missionary after missionary to see the necessity of prayer. His writings always point to God's Word, Jesus Christ, the Holy Spirit, and God the Father.

There have been very few who have had such a depth of understanding of spiritual matters as well as the gift of communicating that understanding to the church. E. M. Bounds was such a man. It was while reading his book *Preacher and Prayer* that I was touched by God to focus my ministry on prayer, revival, and evangelism.

I yielded myself to the blessed task of years of study and research into the life of E. M. Bounds. It is an honor for me, a farm boy from Missouri, saved by grace and called into God's blessed ministry, to share with you a brief overview and insight into what God has done through one man's life.

1

Family Foundation

God shapes the world by prayers. Prayers are deathless. The lips that uttered them may have closed in death, the heart that felt them may have ceased to beat, but the prayers outlive the lives of an age, outlive a world. That man is most immortal who has done the most and best praying. They are God's heroes, God's saints, God's servants, God's vicegerents.

—E. M. Bounds

Edward McKendree Bounds grew up with five brothers and sisters in the small town of Shelbyville, Missouri, a place whose history is filled with the breath of his father, Thomas Jefferson (T. J.) Bounds. In 1835 the Shelby County Commissioners selected a section of land in the center of the county to locate the county seat. T. J. mapped out the town and organized it by December of that year. On March 31, 1836, when Edward was only nine months old, the people gathered in the newly formed town of Shelbyville. The mood was festive as T. J. Bounds sold the lots at a public auction, and before the day was done, he had also purchased one of the lots. The Bounds family was outgrowing their little cabin by the Salt River, and most of T. J.'s business was conducted in town, so he set about to build the family a new home.

11

The Christians had a strong influence in the community, both politically and socially. In 1836 T. J. helped establish the first Temperance Society in Missouri. He and a handful of others put together a strong campaign to eliminate liquor in the county. It was very effective, and Shelby County became a dry county. The Spirit of God ran like a river throughout the region.

The small town was without a formal church but met in regular prayer meetings, Bible studies, and area "preaching days." After two years the Methodist Episcopal Church members joined together and conducted a "camp meeting" with assistance from preachers in neighboring counties. Rev. Richard Sharp, a Methodist, and Rev. Henry Louthan, a Baptist, were mightily used of God during this meeting. There was a great response, and the camp meeting brought about a burden for constant spiritual leadership for the county. The Methodists seized the opportunity, and the first formal Methodist Bible class began in the spring of 1839, from which the First Methodist Church was built a year later. The church was constructed of brick and stood on the top of a lovely little knoll. There, overlooking this growing town, the church became a powerful beacon for all to see.

In May 1840 God added to the Bounds family a third daughter. The family was thrilled with this dainty blessing. Frances and Harriet, ages fourteen and twelve, and Thomas, Charles, and Edward, ages eleven, nine, and five, were all proud to take their new sister, Ellen Sarah, to worship with them in the brand new church building.

The church grew and prospered, and God prospered the Bounds family as well. T. J. was involved in the building and running of the first hotel in Shelbyville, the Smith City Hotel, which served the city for years. He also built a mill to provide needed flour for the community.

As agriculture rapidly became the leading industry in the heartland of America, it soon became apparent that an organization was needed to give support, encouragement, education, and financial assistance to the farmers. T. J. Bounds helped to form a county agricultural society and was selected to draft a constitution for the organization. This document became one of the leading models for the formulation of agricultural societies across Missouri, Kansas, and Iowa. He also served in many political areas of the city, including clerk of the county and the court.

April 1849 marked the arrival of the family's first grandchild. Harriet and her husband, the Reverend William Vandeventer, had a precious baby girl, Mary. But the joy was tempered by the fact that William had tragically fallen ill during the harsh Missouri winter. He had been working in the snow building a barn and became sick with a flu-like illness that turned into pneumonia. He died in May, after seven months of great agony. Young Edward was particularly affected by the loss because "Uncle" William had become quite a friend and encourager to him.

As his wealth increased, T. J. assisted many of the townspeople with short-term loans that enabled them to build. Homes were erected in the city, and the countryside was filled with even more homes, new roads, crops, and cattle. People were drawn to settle where they could raise their families with new hope. Businesses were built, and soon the city's courthouse was bustling with activity. T. J. Bounds could always be found in the midst of this growth. The county hired him to erect a fence to protect the landscape around the courthouse. Many would tie their horses and wagons right up to the building rather than leave them in the street, and the county wanted to discourage this practice. While working on the fence for the courthouse, T. J. was stricken with tuberculosis.

On September 13, 1849, at the age of forty-four,

Thomas Jefferson Bounds entered into the presence of his Savior and Friend, Jesus Christ. He was buried in the rolling hillside of the city cemetery. It was at his father's funeral, at the age of fourteen, that Edward began his spiritual search.

T. J. Bounds was a man of integrity. He had prepared well for his family, and his estate left them in good provision. His life holdings consisted of much land, buildings, and the reimbursement of money from those who had borrowed from him. His personal belongings included Bibles, books, and other educational materials, which were appropriated to Edward. His teaching and good example were a strong influence on his children and prepared them for service to their Lord.

2

Seeking

Waiting, waiting; 'tis so far
To the day that is to come;
One by one the days that are
All to tell their countless sum;
Each to dawn and each to die,
What is so far as by and by?
Waiting, waiting; 'tis not ours,
This today that flies so fast;
Let them go, the shadowy hours,
Floating, floated, into past.
One day wears tomorrow's sky—
What is so near as by and by?

—Augusta Webster

The funeral services were over, and life went on at the Bounds' home. The absence of father and husband left an incredible void, even in the full household. Edward's mother seemed a bit lost without his father's strong arm of support. His sister Harriet, who had lost her own husband, seemed best able to offer the comfort and empathy their mother needed. Thomas, the oldest brother, would assume his father's responsibilities. This was a heavy load but one for which Thomas had been well prepared.

With word spreading throughout the country of the tremendous veins of gold being mined in California, Charles spent much time talking with their cousin John Bird. John and his children had decided to join the caravans heading west. Many were selling all they had in hopes of making an easy fortune in the gold mines. Charles was excited about the idea and had decided to join the Birds on their trip. Because Charles and Edward were close, Charles wanted Edward to go with them. It was a bold step for a young man of fourteen to leave his home and travel thousands of miles into unknown territory but Edward was quite mature, and he realized the opportunity was a good one; the risk to someone with as few responsibilities as he and Charles had was slim. He would arrange to travel with his brother and his cousin's family to the gold mines of the West.

Preparations were quickly made as the young men received their mother's blessing and the encouragement of their brothers and sisters on their venture. Edward and Charles said their good-byes and began their journey. The group had to stop briefly in Platte County, Missouri, and while there they visited relatives John and Elizabeth Bounds. To their surprise, John and Elizabeth were packing their belongings getting ready to travel westward also—not for gold but for the free land being given away in Oregon. They aligned themselves with a wagon train headed for North Platte, Nebraska, where the group remained for the winter.

As the snow melted, the travelers continued, and by spring Edward and Charles found themselves in a desolate California canyon called Mesquite. They were excited as they entered the rugged gold mining camp of Placerville, in Eldorado County, where Charles passed his seventeenth birthday, and Edward his fifteenth.

But their excitement quickly turned to hard work, and the boys labored diligently. They were appalled at the degradation around them as they observed their fellow miners spending their spare time in saloons and gambling halls. The filth of the camp reminded both Edward and Charles that "the love of money is the root of all evil." They had seen their father acquire much wealth, yet he had never loved money. On the contrary, the men around them sank lower and lower, until not only did they love money and drift from the faith but they seemed to "pierce themselves through with many sorrows." Perhaps it was here in the gold mines that Edward first resolved to never let money or possessions gain importance in his life. He would vow to follow "after righteousness, godliness, faith, love, patience, meekness" (1 Tim. 6:10–11).

After four years with little success, the brothers left the mines and headed for home. Years later it was said of the Bounds brothers that they were perhaps the only people to ever return from the gold mines with their faith greater than it was before they left.

St. Louis was a flurry of activity. Edward and Charles Bounds sat at the edge of the mighty Mississippi, glad to be back in Missouri, with their futures ahead of them. The barges moving up and down the river seemed to give Charles inspiration, and he began what would become a very successful freight business.

Edward had always been fascinated by his father's political dealings, and his decision was to go into law. In the spring of 1854 Edward left St. Louis, and his brother Charles, and went to Hannibal to study.

The knowledge Edward had gleaned from his father, along with his keen intelligence, enabled him to progress rapidly in his studies and to be installed, at the age of nineteen, as the state's youngest lawyer. He set up practice in Hannibal, where he served for three years.

But it was not in God's plan for Edward to remain in the law business. Instead, He would call him to impact the world through his preaching and writing. Ironically, a few miles downriver from Shelbyville, another child was born the same year as Edward that would also impact the country through his writing. His name was Samuel Clemens, known in the literary world as Mark Twain.

3

The Call

The preacher on whom God's power descends must be marked by loyalty to God's Word. The Holy Ghost cannot and will not sanction by his approval disloyalty to God's Word. The preacher must accept and act on the statement that "God has magnified His Word above all His name." And he must hold God's Word in this high and unchallenged eminence and never veer from it.

—E. M. Bounds

In 1857 America was growing and changing. The Mexican War was over, and prosperity seemed to be the order of the day. But God almighty knew what tragedy and despair lay ahead for this country and He needed His people to be renewed and strengthened.

The fires of revival spread up and down the eastern seaboard and then moved westward into the heart of the country as the Great Spiritual Awakening of 1857–1858 burst full force. City after city received the testimony of God's mighty convicting power as the consuming fire of the Holy Spirit purged the church of the dross of unconfessed sin. As God's people began to pray, the heathen began to respond to the holy conviction of the Spirit of God, and the churches were filled as never before.

As Edward sat in his Hannibal law office pondering

the condition of his city and his own soul, he read letters from friends and family concerning a stirring among God's people in the East. Even people in Chicago, with all its corruption, had begun turning to God. The Methodist reports spoke of a revival at Keokuk, Iowa, a few miles north of Hannibal, where over six thousand souls had been converted in two months.

As autumn leaves began to fall and the countryside was bathed in rich hues of gold and red, God continued His work up and down the Mississippi River. Evangelist Smith Thomas planned to hold a meeting in a small river port city just north of Hannibal, called LaGrange.

The churches in town were not large enough to contain the meetings, so the people of the Methodist Episcopal Church became the seedbed for the construction of a brush arbor on the banks of the Mississippi, across the street from the church. It was here that Brother Smith Thomas began his series of meetings.

The Spirit of God moved mightily in E. M. Bounds. He knew the time had come to give up his practice and his law books to study and prepare for the higher work of God. Just as the mighty Mississippi flowed unrestrained downstream, Bounds gave up control of his life and submitted to the call of almighty God. "I press toward the mark for the prize of the high calling of God in Christ Jesus" (Phil. 3:14).

Back in Hannibal, he quickly concluded his business and moved north to the small hamlet of Palmyra, Missouri. Here, among the rolling hills of this small community, was located the Centenary Seminary of the First Methodist Episcopal Church South. This was the place God indicated Edward begin his formal training for the ministry.

After two years of diligent study and prayer, Bounds applied for trial approval at the 1860 Methodist Episcopal Church South Conference. Because of his long years of exposure to the Methodist Church and the reputation of his parents, Edward became noted in the region. His analytical mind vigorously grasped the Word of God, and his faith allowed him to develop a pious conviction that would follow him throughout his ministry. His years in law practice had also trained him to be quite proficient in speaking before an audience.

At the Hannibal Quarterly Conference, on February 21, 1860, Bounds preached to pastors. His style had become bold and fervent. Even the presence of his family did not deter him from delivering a stern and forceful message. At the conclusion of the conference, a unanimous decision was reached to recommend Bounds to the Methodist Episcopal Church South. The letter of recognition was even more precious to young Bounds because it was signed by Reverend Cornelius Vandevender, who was the presiding elder and his sister's father-in-law.

Edward was thrilled to receive his ministerial assignment. He was to cover the Monticello circuit, which had been his pastor's, the Reverend E. M. Marvin. Monticello was a few miles north, and the wintry ride awaited him. He would have time to talk with God and gather direction for the people he would shepherd.

4

The War Begins

Good Christians are the best in every station. In address-
ing a lot of new recruits at the time they were sworn into
the army, the Emperor William took occasion to observe
that no one could be a good soldier who was not a good
Christian, and that the recruits who took the oath of al-
legiance to their earthly master should also, and above
all things, "prove themselves true to their heavenly Lord."

—E. M. Bounds

For a year Edward Bounds moved from town to farm
over the rugged roads of the Monticello circuit. He held
prayer meetings and Bible studies throughout the region, and the people responded and grew spiritually.
Bounds' preaching was stern, powerful, and compelling,
and the circuit grew in numbers as well. Often the young
bachelor would be given chickens, corn, or a bag of peas,
as his flock shared their bounty with their shepherd.
Brother Bounds knew the labor and toil that went into
each harvest and he was indeed thankful that his people
were willing to share the fruits of their labor with him.

The enthusiasm Bounds had for God and His Word
spilled over, and the people were influenced toward God
in a mighty way. His organizational and administrative
abilities, combined with the power of God, allowed him

to do the work of three men. He prepared the region to establish a Bible school in the Monticello church, and this was accomplished by his successor. Bounds also began a seminary, or a church school, which later became very influential in the region. This school left a legacy of the teachings of E. M. Bounds and also taught the basics of education, reading, writing, and arithmetic. Bounds believed in emphasizing discipline that led people into discipleship, but he did not pressure them into submission.

Bounds' future looked bright and promising. But on April 12, 1861, word came that shots had been fired at Fort Sumter.

These initial shots spread across the country, sounding loudly in Missouri. The noise was disturbing to Brother Bounds. "A sound of battle is in the land, and of great destruction" (Jer. 50:22).

Missouri was a state already annoyed with the Federal government because of the position it held during Missouri's quest for statehood. Yet the leadership of the state was poor and would never firmly take a stand either for or against the Union. The people of the state, however, became more and more sympathetic toward the Confederacy as the war proceeded.

Shortly after the skirmish at Fort Sumter, Edward looked forward to a trip to St. Louis. His brother Charles had fallen deeply in love with a young lady from Louisiana, Missouri, and their wedding would take place on April 23, 1861. It was good to see the family, and the wedding was a festive celebration, but worry and fear for the future of the nation seemed to hang like a fog over the entire gathering.

The fear was valid, for shortly after the wedding, on May 10, 1861, the St. Louis Massacre occurred. The Confederate-sympathizing State Guard was protecting the arsenal at St. Louis. The Union troops, outnumbering the State Guard with about 7,000 men, and led by General Lyons, marched in and took the arsenal, making prisoners of the State Guard. The Guard had no choice but to surrender, being so completely outnumbered and outgunned.

That afternoon, as they marched the prisoners through the streets, a crowd of men, women, and children gathered and began to taunt the Union troops. The troops retaliated by firing into the crowd. Twenty-eight people were killed, mostly civilians, including a baby in its mothers arms. Two men who witnessed this hideous crime would later play important roles in the struggle for the country. They were William T. Sherman and Ulysses S. Grant.

Though the incident only increased the support of the Confederate cause by the people of Missouri, the government tried to remain neutral. The St. Louis Massacre had put the state into a condition of war, however, and political temperatures were high. General Lyons was considered a murderer by the people of Missouri, although he blamed the entire ordeal on the German and Irish civilians who taunted the Union troops that afternoon.

In September, during the Missouri Methodist Episcopal Church South Conference, disturbing news was announced. Edward Bounds found it particularly unsettling and he again questioned his feelings about the war. His friends Rev. E. E. Miller and E. M. Marvin had gone from Missouri to New Orleans, Louisiana, to attend the National Conference of the Methodist Church South, which had been canceled without their knowledge. When they tried to return home, they found themselves in a dilemma. Missouri was controlled by Union forces, and once the men crossed the border they would be in danger of being considered spies. Reverend Miller took his chances and returned home. But as soon as he crossed the Missouri River, he was arrested and imprisoned, where he remained until the end of the war.

Reverend Marvin remained in the South, and seeing a need for chaplains in the army, he sought out his friend Gen. Sterling Price and joined the Confederate Army. He started "The Army Church," which had an "Articles of Faith" and a "Church Constitution."

At the Missouri Conference, Bounds was surprised to receive a new assignment. The Brunswick Station had formerly been pastored by Rev. William G. Caples, the presiding elder at the conference. This was a well-established church, which stood on a hillside overlooking the Missouri River. Reverend Caples was known far and wide for the intense two-week debate he held with Rev. Moses E. Lard, a very gifted expounder of the Christian church. The debate was moderated by ex-governor Sterling Price, and crowds of nearly 1,500 came from across the nation to hear these two great men debate in the largest open area in the community, a tobacco warehouse. At the end of the debate, both sides claimed victory. Observers said little changed due to the debate. In fact, everyone adhered even more to their favored and respected creeds and doctrines. Caples was looking for someone of great spiritual depth to take this church, which he loved and where his own wife's family would be. The ministry fell to young E. M. Bounds.

Late in October, the countryside ablaze with color as the hardwood leaves announced the arrival of autumn, Edward arrived in Brunswick, Missouri. This was a town growing rapidly both in numbers and prestige but was a community torn asunder by a recent battle a few miles away, in Lexington. There Union troops had fought against Missouri troops sympathetic to the State Guard and the Confederacy. Brunswick was also the hometown of Confederate Gen. Sterling Price, and the talk was centered on the war almost to the exclusion of all else.

Edward Bounds saw more of his fellow-laborers for Christ forced to take a stand, many joining the Confederates as Reverend Marvin had done. The war and all it represented plagued Edward. His family had owned slaves in the past but theirs was a different situation than the norm. In the summer of 1830 Edward's father had been in the city square and happened to observe a slave auction. One young woman had obviously been abused, and her mother stood beside her with a look of fear and desperation, knowing that soon she would be separated from her daughter. T. J. Bounds took compassion on them and signed an agreement that allowed him to "rent" the mother and daughter, Dinah and Maria, from their owners. Edward's mother, Hatty, treated them as her own family and they lived together in harmony. Dinah soon adopted the Bounds' surname as her own. The only disadvantage to keeping the women was that outsiders would think the Bounds family approved of the practice of slavery. But God knew their hearts.

Edward had never seen savagery in the owning of slaves, only the same kindness that Maria and Dinah were shown. Yet he knew such cruelty existed. He also despised the greed that went along with the merchandising of human life. Slavery was wrong both in the southern cotton fields and in the northern factories, known as human sweat shops. But the war wasn't being fought over slavery alone, particularly not in Missouri.

While questions and struggles over issues such as slavery filled Edward's mind, he had no such questions when it came to the subject of a state's right to secede. He was absolutely sure that any state had the constitutional right. He had studied *Rawle's View of the Consti-*

tution during his preparation as a lawyer, and it clearly identified the rights of the state. He also knew that the leaders in Washington were well aware of this legal truth because it was taught at military institutions such as West Point.

Greed and power were what the war was truly being fought over. And it was this fact that angered Edward the most. He had never been able to tolerate this position when Jesus Christ so clearly taught against it, yet he saw it on both sides of the war. The Confederates were unwilling to lose money by giving freedom to human beings and paying them an honest wage. The Union was threatened by the ability of the South to trade more easily as the railroads opened the markets of the West and the Mississippi River ports opened trade routes north and south. *Greed.* "The desire of the slothful killeth him; for his hands refuse to labour. He coveteth greedily all the day long: but the righteous giveth and spareth not" (Prov. 21:25–26).

5

Persecution and Prison

Charles Bounds, brother and confidant, could already foresee that he could not continue his business along the Mississippi River. He sent Edward testimonials of the immoral and vicious practices going on around him. His religious convictions would not allow him to condone such acts. The great river was strategic in the war effort and as such would make his business too dangerous, not only for Charles but for the men who worked with him. Charles could not see himself joining the cause of either side of the war, so he and Margaret moved to Oregon to begin a new life. The war affected everyone, and Edward, though a minister of the gospel, was no exception.

As Edward continued to preach submission to those in authority, even in the Federal government, his soul was troubled by the actions of those in authority in Missouri. Union forces ravaged the area, inflicting great cruelty on many. In one incident a seventeen-year-old youth, John Lenard, was accused of being a bushwhacker and was taken by the Union soldiers to the frozen Grand River and held under the water until he died. It was a sad and mournful day when E. M. Bounds preached the

young boy. Many suffered under such Un-
ifty-five noncombatants were executed in
egion by Union soldiers attempting to de-
˽aynawkers and Confederate sympathizers.
˽till, Bounds continued in the Lord's work, and in June
1862 he wrote in his quarterly conference report that the
Brunswick Station Church was averaging seventy people
in attendance.

In September the state of Missouri was placed under
martial law. The Missourians were furious as Union provost marshals were given absolute authority over them.
On September 12, 1862, Gen. R. Curtis was placed in
command of the state of Missouri. General Curtis had recently lost his son, Maj. H. Z. Curtis, in a skirmish with
Quatral's raiders. This loss was like a poison, and its
venom lashed out at anyone suspected of being a Confederate sympathizer. Many serving under General Curtis
disagreed with his tactics and felt the martial law order
was uncalled for.

These latest actions compelled many north Missourians to embrace the Confederacy all the more. As the war
moved closer and closer to home, an incident in Palmyra
had a great impact on Edward Bounds.

In the early days of October, just as the cold was start-
ing to set in, Confederate Gen. Joe Porter was marching
through the city of Palmyra, in Edward's region. A small
garrison of Union forces was occupying the courthouse.
General Porter decided to take their arms, and a battle
ensued. The city's terrain made the Methodist church,
where Brother Bounds had attended, the perfect place to
use for fortifications and firing down upon the courthouse.

This act angered Provost Marshal Stracham, who was
already vowing vengeance because of Confederate vio-
lence against some of his supporters. On October 18,
1862, Stracham, often referred to as "the Beast," selected

ten men, falsely accused of being Gen. Joe Porter's troops, to be executed publicly by hanging. These citizens were executed without trial or hearing before a military court. One young woman pleaded with "the Beast" for her husband's life. Stracham required sex in exchange for his life, and after this desperate young woman complied with his ungodly demands, Stracham commanded her to choose another man to take her husband's place. The anguished woman could not ask another innocent man to die. But a youth, with no wife or child, who knew what had transpired, volunteered and gave his life. He asked only that his mother be informed that he died honorably. His mother asked her former pastor to preach the boy's funeral. E. M. Bounds returned with haste to minister to the grieving family of this gallant young man.

After this brutal act, it was revealed that none of the ten men had had anything to do with General Porter or his troops. Because Stracham had ultimate authority, the "Palmyra Massacre" passed into history without any rebuff to those committing the crimes. The only inquiry into the matter, occurring much later, would find falsified documents trying to justify the hanging of ten innocent men.

Edward knew the people of Palmyra. He had pastored many of the families of the men hanged. Without justice, E. M. Bounds, the pastor, the lawyer, and the Christian struggled with submission to authority that did not submit to the higher authority of God. Was civil disobedience allowed in God's Word when there was such blatant misuse of power?

As the weather turned colder, the Missouri countryside remained troubled. The Confederates were seeking supplies and recruits. The Union army was seeking further revenge. Guerrilla forces were seeking plunder. The citizens were nervous—never knowing who might come to their door.

On November 14, 1862, a list was composed of 250 men who were to be apprehended and given opportunity to pledge an Oath of Allegiance to the Union. They would also have to post a $500 bond to be released. Bounds' name appeared on the list. The church at Brunswick Station was a part of the Methodist Episcopal Church South. Any organization or church with "south" in its title was considered suspect to the Confederacy. Even though this was strictly a geographical description, Bounds and other pastors were considered offenders. Quite often this persecution came from the denomination of the North, which was still bitter over the split into both "Methodist South" and "Southern Baptists" that had stemmed from the slavery issue. This convinced Brother Bounds that denominational organizations could be more of a political power struggle than a spiritual body, if allowed.

The bond money was, in actuality, a way for Union forces to raise funds to replace railroads, bridges, etc. that had been destroyed in battle by the Union troops, Confederate troops, and Jayhawkers. When these roads were destroyed, it was up to civilians to replace them, though such replacement would always benefit the troops as much if not more than the civilian populace. Bounds did not have the bond money to begin with but was also morally against the principle of the Union's raising money in this way.

J. A. Merchant, Superintendent of the Brunswick Methodist Episcopal South Church Bible School, gave the following account of his attempts to persuade Bounds to give allegiance to the Union army:

> In 1862 he was banished South for refusing to take the prescribed oath, which was required of ministers in these war times. I insisted upon his remaining and taking the oath, as he was a frail and delicate man, and I was fearful that he could not stand the hardship before him, but he persisted in going South, and I fitted him

with a pair of brogan boots and other supplies, and off he went for "Dixie."

Bounds had found himself at the deciding point at last. He could see no reason to be asked to pledge an oath to the Union when he was an American citizen. The Union needed the clergy on their side to retain control of the communities, and Bounds knew this was a political attempt to "buy" him. If he agreed, his people would realize this as well and his influence with them would be lost. If he did not agree, his influence would still be lost, for this would mean his arrest by the Union army.

Bounds was indeed arrested along with 249 others. In the cold of winter, without provisions or extra clothing, they were placed on the open cargo deck of a steamship and transferred to Jefferson City. There they were thrown in the stockade and held below the state capitol on the water's edge. When the group became larger, they were taken by train to Jefferson Barracks in St. Louis. Trains were so packed there was scarcely room to stand. Ironically, Jefferson Barracks was the same general location where some twenty-five years earlier a young Robert E. Lee had been stationed while helping to save sections of St. Louis from the river. Lee's house was only a few short blocks from the location where Bounds was now held prisoner.

Once in St. Louis, the prisoners were taken to a place that had come to be known as Lynch's Slave Pit. Formerly the Garrett Street Medical College, this location was disgraced and decimated when the Union army turned it into a prison because the institution's founder, Dr. Joseph McDowell, was a southern sympathizer.

At Lynch's Slave Pit, Bounds found the conditions a thousand times worse than the primitive gold mining camps in California. Here in the prison the cells were so crowded there was no room for the people to lie down or rest. The men would lean against the wall and brace their feet against each other in order to sleep in a standing position. Women were confined and physically and sexually assaulted by the soldiers, oftentimes in front of their husbands. Food was taken from the riverfront, most of it vegetables that had been thrown away because they were unfit to eat. Plates and utensils were never washed but handed from one person to the next in the short time allowed for eating.

The tragedy was that most of these prisoners were noncombatants, innocent of any impropriety against the government. They had not been tried or convicted of any crime but arrested on suspicion of the possibility of Confederate support. Many of those in charge of this calamity claimed a spiritual heritage to Jesus Christ and His command to "love your enemy." Yet they treated not only the enemy in such a brutal way but also these innocent victims suspected of disloyalty to their cause.

On December 1, 1862, Rev. W. G. Eliot, along with Dr. W. N. Reeves, pastor of the First Baptist Church of St. Louis, wrote to President Lincoln protesting the arrest of ministers because the word "south" appeared in the church name and because they objected to the imposing of levy and bond for suspected secessionists. In their letter, they proposed the arrests were an illegal infringement upon the people both of the United States and the state of Missouri, and that it was not permitted even under martial law. In fact, there were constitutional questions throughout the entire process. A copy of the letter was sent to General Curtis.

Still seeking recourse in the death of his son, General Curtis was only antagonized by the letter. And as the letter and the clergy involved became a great focus between Missouri and President Lincoln, Curtis became even more hostile.

The weather that December was extremely harsh.

The temperatures dropped into the low teens and ice and snow were common. During this dreadful and despairing time, Bounds did his best to encourage those around him. He sang, prayed, and tried to remain a joyful presence for the sake of others. He requested to hold a Christmas worship service in the prison to celebrate the Savior's birth and share some hope during this time of catastrophe. His request was denied.

On December 31, 1862, Maj. Gen. Sam Curtis enacted the Banishment Order 23. On the same day, provost marshal, Gen. Lieut. F. A. Dick of St. Louis, signed a special order requiring Brother Bounds to leave Missouri and not to return until the rebellion ceased. He was ordered behind the combat lines of the Confederacy.

Bounds was taken back to Jefferson Barracks to be transported to Memphis, Tennessee, and then to Arkansas. Three days after Bounds' banishment, President Lincoln sent word that the mistreatment of ministers was to be stopped, and General Curtis was reprimanded. Unfortunately, it was three days too late.

Bounds was placed on a ship laden with supplies for General Grant. Locked in security, he was unable to move around on the boat. Though weak, without heat, little food, and still imprisoned, Bounds took his example from Silas and the apostle Paul, praising God by singing hymns of Wesley. The troops, mostly of English and Irish descent, questioned Bounds on his joy during such trying circumstances, giving him the opportunity to share Jesus Christ with these men who were heading into battle. Many were out for financial gain, their futures grim, and Bounds offered them true gain and secure futures through redemption in the Savior. "For though I be free from all men, yet have I made myself servant unto all, that I might gain the more" (1 Cor. 9:19).

Shortly after embarking for Memphis, Bounds learned that he would have to go even farther south.

Grant had started his push for Vicksburg. On January 7, 1863, under orders from General Tuttle, Bounds was released to travel on toward Memphis on a river barge laden with supplies for Grant's siege of Vicksburg. Chaos reigned in Memphis, as frenzied troops were preparing for Grant's siege, and General Sherman's troops were desperately trying to reestablish the rear echelon after a devastating defeat a few miles north.

Eventually Bounds was sent by train to Washington, Arkansas, in the south-central area of the state, to a prisoner exchange camp. Washington, Arkansas, was often referred to as "Missouri in exile" because many of those who had fled Missouri had come and set up a camp or tent village there. In this camp, Bounds fellowshiped with many friends and relatives of families back home. The officer in charge of the camp, Col. J. E. Glynn, was at a loss as to what to do with this small, frail, noncombatant preacher of the Gospel that seemed to radiate Jesus Christ. Bounds learned of the war actions in Mississippi and also heard that his friend Gen. Sterling Price was there. A desire burned deep within Bounds' soul to join General Price in Mississippi. On February 20, 1863, Colonel Glynn gave Bounds a pass through lines of war to secure his safe passage to the southern states. He had received his release from bondage but still had to face the requirements of the banishment order.

He began to walk eastward, going through the picket lines of the Union forces, trying to reach Tupelo, Mississippi, where he believed General Price could be found. Weak from the cold, he walked over 200 miles before reaching the small town of Pinebluff, Arkansas. There he struck a deal with a Methodist farmer who agreed to sell him a mule for $200, which Bounds would pay after the war was ended—if he lived through it.

Once he had acquired the mule, Bounds continued southeast, following the Arkansas River. Crossing a channel to a small island, he traversed one of the few shallow parts of the river over into Mississippi. From there he headed due east. In Greenwood, he was told that most of the Missouri troops were northeast of him, near Holly Springs, but General Price's men were back on the other side of the Mississippi, merging to defend Vicksburg. Bounds abandoned his faithful mule and obtained passage on the Great Northern train. He got as far as Abbeville, Mississippi, before the train was turned around to take supplies back toward Jackson. Bounds got off the train in Abbeville, and began to walk to Camp Pritchard, just southeast of Holly Springs, where the Missouri troops were camped.

Realizing his pursuit of General Price could be in vain, and seeing the valor and spirit of the Missouri Third, on February 7, 1863, at the age of twenty-eight, Edward McKendree Bounds joined the Confederate army. He was assigned to the Missouri Third Infantry Company B, under command of General Bowen.

6

The Action

Should Sorrow lay her hand upon thy shoulder,
And walk with thee in silence on life's way,
While joy, thy bright companion once, grows colder,
Becomes more distant day by day;
Shrink not from the companionship of Sorrow,
She is the messenger of God to thee;
And thou wilt thank Him in His great tomorrow.
For what thou knowest not now thou then shalt see;
She is God's angel, clad in weeds of night,
With whom "we walk by faith, and not by sight."

—E. M. Bounds

Chaplain E. M. Bounds quickly settled into military life. Many among the Missouri troops inquired of home, and Bounds gave any news he could. He enjoyed the reunion with many friends and acquaintances, especially with his dear friend and father in the ministry, E. M. Marvin, who would later become a bishop.

Conversations with the other chaplains often reflected on the revival that swept the troops after their defeat at Iuka, Mississippi. In September 1862, while in full retreat just east of Tupelo, God opened heaven on the troops—with repentance, conversions, and numerous commitments to the church. The Union forces had disengaged their pursuit down the Natchez Trace without apparent reason. It was as if a curtain had been drawn over the retreating troops as God breathed upon them in a spiritual revival. The statement "Prayer is the foundation for revival, testimony is the fuel" proved true. In one meeting alone there were forty men who embraced the Savior through the preaching of Dr. B. T. Kavanaugh.

One man who had a great impact on E. M. Bounds during the war held quite different convictions in his service to God. The man was Father John B. Bannon, often called the "fighting Catholic chaplain." Bannon believed his place should be at the front of the battle, not in the rear echelon where most chaplains served. Bannon saw that it was those men who were most seriously wounded and dying that had the greatest need of one who could point them to God.

On February 28, 1863, Bounds received word that General Price, the commander of the old Missouri Home Guard, would be relocated to the west side of the Mississippi River, where he would become the general of all forces on that side, as was his desire. An agreement had been made with President Jefferson Davis to allow Price to make this move because he was familiar with the terrain and the fighting tactics in that area and felt he would be most effective there. Though all Missouri troops were supposed to return with General Price, President Davis reviewed the situation and realized that they were too valuable in their current position, as General Grant was moving south toward Vicksburg. As a result, only the immediate staff and a few chaplains were transferred.

On March 10, 1863, orders came for all remaining troops to move to Vicksburg. During the march, the people of the small town of Linden came out to greet them, welcoming the troops. As word spread that the soldiers were from Missouri, and hadn't been home for a long time, the hearts of the townspeople were touched. They offered their homes to the weary men, and many of the grateful soldiers accepted their hospitality and enjoyed a home-cooked meal.

Later that evening, many soldiers and townspeople gathered in a small Methodist church to hear Chaplain Bounds share the Word of God. He preached, sang, and prayed, and the portholes of heaven were opened and the Spirit of God sent an outpouring that bathed their receptive hearts. "And from Jesus Christ, who is the faithful witness, and the first begotten of the dead, and the prince of the kings of the earth. Unto him that loved us, and washed us from our sins in his own blood" (Rev. 1:5). Among those touched that evening was Gen. Martin E. Green of the Second Division of the Missouri Army.

Two days later the brigade's camp was established about two miles from Grand Gulf on a well-suited flat field. Upon establishing a headquarters, Bounds was presented with his reassignment orders to General Green's division. General Green was already in command of a portion of the Arkansas army that had not returned to Arkansas with General Price. He assigned Brother Bounds to the First Sharp Shooters of the Arkansas Volunteers.

When he arrived at his new charge, Bounds found two of his cousins, Benjamin H. Bounds and Alonzo M. Bounds, from St. Francis County, Arkansas. Both had been captured at the battle of Shiloh. They shared the news that another cousin, Thomas J. Bounds, had been killed at Corinth. Thomas's brother, Thetas, along with Richard Dozier Bounds were both recuperating from wounds received in the battle of Corinth, and were in Vicksburg. Edward began to realize while comforting these two men just how large the Bounds family was and that it extended from Missouri to Mississippi, Arkansas to Tennessee.

In Grand Gulf, Edward found the environment much like Hannibal. The night air was filled with the loud music of hoot howls, bullfrogs, and crickets. Many of the men seemed bothered by the noise, but for the men from the river areas, it was the sound of home. In the evenings the men would gig frogs and then enjoy fried frog legs. Also supplementing the troops rations was hearty rabbit meat from the large swamp rabbits that were plentiful in the region.

Their time at Grand Gulf was short because General Grant decided to move Union forces around Vicksburg and attack it from the south, where the terrain was more level. Grant placed Maj. Gen. John McClernan in charge of this maneuver, and these troops began to make their way by the Louisiana side of Vicksburg.

At about the same time, from their post at Grand Gulf, Col. Frances Mearon Cockrell was sent with his fighting Missouri troops to assist the Fifteenth Battalion Louisiana Cavalry. Colonel Cockrell was from Warrensburg, Missouri, where he, like Bounds, had practiced law. Cockrell was also a staunch Christian and member of the Methodist Episcopal Church South. Though it is unlikely that these men crossed paths before this time, they soon became close companions, with much in common. (Cockrell was elected to Congress after the war and vehemently fought against alcohol and influence peddling. He was an enemy of the carpetbagger and others trying to exploit the misfortune of anyone during reconstruction.)

On April 4 the steamboats ferried Colonel Cockrell and the First and Second Missouri Infantries, with support, across the Mississippi River. The next day Chaplain Bounds and the Third Missouri Infantry also crossed to join Cockrell. These three regiments obtained a good position just south of Bayou Vidal, in order to stop McClearon's Federal advance. The valiant efforts of the Missouri troops held the Federal troops at bay for thirteen days. After nearly two weeks of fighting in the delta swampland, the Missouri troops returned to Hard Times

Landing and crossed the Mississippi River back to Grand Gulf.

Just a short time later the battle plans became clear for the taking of Vicksburg, as the Union forces brought the ironclads down the river to Hard Times Landing. On April 29 Grant started the bombardment of the fortifications on the eastern shore, including the Fort of Grand Gulf.

During this shelling, E. M. Bounds experienced the hell of war on the battlefield. The Arkansas Sharpshooters had been deployed at a strategic location in the advent of a landing at Fort Gibson, and to combat the sniper fire from the ships. About nine o'clock one of the cannon rounds hit the rifle pit, killing and wounding more than eleven men. General Green called in the Missouri Third, and they merged to defend the sector. During this experience, Bounds determined that, like Father Bannon, he would remain at the front lines of battle. He wanted to be where fear, pain, and death lingered with the men. "For they cried to God in battle, and he was entreated of them; because they put their trust in him" (1 Chron. 5:20). There were others who could help in the rear echelons to offer comfort, pray for healing, and help those who remained to deal with their grief for their fallen comrades.

Because of the ferocious resistance around Grand Gulf, and incorrect information given to him, General Grant decided not to attempt the crossing of the Mississippi at Hard Times Landing but sent the forces farther south about four miles. There at the Disharoon Plantation the troops spent the night.

On April 30 the Union forces started to cross the river into Mississippi at Bruinsburg. General Green was dispatched to Port Gibson. By late afternoon camp and perimeter were set two miles west of town and ten miles from Bruinsburg. These troops stood directly between the Union army and their objective. Just before dark the troops of both forces met in a skirmish that caused General McPherson to send an emergency report to General Grant. Grant then stopped the advance for the night. That evening, at a little church, Bounds conducted services. The small building was packed beyond standing-room capacity. The singing, praying, and preaching lasted until past the midnight hour.

The dawn of May 1 proved to be costly. Fighting began at first light and did not conclude until darkness blurred the vision of the soldiers. Bounds spent that evening, not in a church but in the wooded battlefield, going from one soldier to another. This little man of great faith prayed with the dying, gave aid to the suffering, inspiration to those of faith, and courage to those who were afraid. When the black of night pulled over them like a window shade, and the tragedy and suffering could no longer be seen, only the cries of agony mingled with the deafening silence of the dead. The death angel looked not at the uniform of butternut gray or the blue and gold, but at the crimson blood shed on the battlefield of man. "Continual weeping shall go up; for . . . the enemies have heard a cry of destruction" (Jer. 48:5).

Late in the night the troops left their place of retreat near the suspension bridge that crossed Pierre Bayou. As the bridge burned, Bounds, along with other soldiers, marched north between Pierre Bayou and Big Black River. They made camp at Clear Creek near Bovina, Mississippi, where they would remain for fourteen days awaiting reinforcements.

Bounds, however, would not remain with them. On May 12 the surgeon in charge, M. K. Allian, sent Bounds to Jackson, Mississippi, for supplies. He started out on this mission of mercy with the knowledge that General Grant had defeated the resistance at Raymond and was on his way to Jackson. The Union forces were already closer to the city than Bounds.

At daybreak he headed east along the roadbed of the abandoned southern Mississippi railroad. Traveling along this seldom used route allowed him to arrive in Jackson by late that afternoon. He spent the night in the Methodist College with the remaining faculty and ministerial students. Armed with a fresh supply of Bibles, tracts, newspapers, and books he and his traveling companion went to the hospital in search of medical supplies. They returned that night to the college before beginning their journey back to the troops.

They were awakened by the sound of artillery. The two men made a hasty withdrawal around the Union forces that blocked the railroad and returned to Clear Creek, with the news that Grant had taken the city of Jackson.

On May 15 General Pemberton moved his troops to block General Grant's Union forces, who were moving swiftly toward Vicksburg. These opposing forces met on the Champion Plantation. There among the wooden fence rows, the rolling hills, the stately oaks, and the blooms of the magnolia trees a battle of contrary convictions was held. Colonel Cockrell rode into the fray with his sword in one hand and the reins of his horse and a magnolia blossom in the other. The battle of Champion's Hill was a costly attempt to stop General Grant. The men from Missouri demonstrated their bravery and saved the day. Though General Pemberton had already been impressed by these fighting men, it was here at Champion's Hill that their spirit became dear to his heart.

Bounds was there in the thick of the fighting, and as the troops withdrew to Edward's Station, he worked closely with the wounded. Among the injured he found a dear friend—Col. H. G. McKinney from Boone County, Missouri. He had been wounded in the chest during battle, and Bounds remained with him until the next day when McKinney was lifted into the loving arms of his heavenly Father.

After the battle along the Big Black River, all the Confederate troops were called into the fortifications of Vicksburg. Because of the impression the Missouri troops had made on General Pemberton, he ordered them to be held in reserve to give reinforcement to any breach in fortifications. This was later proven to be an extremely wise decision. This order also made it easier for Bounds to be of help. He was able to preach in many different locations, even within the city of Vicksburg.

Though God was moving in Vicksburg, many of the Confederate chaplains decided to get out of the city. They felt sure Grant would succeed and they feared defeat. Bounds was led by his convictions to stay. How could he preach the sufficiency of Christ and run from the threat of suffering? His understanding of human nature was accurate. As the chaplains left, it caused many soldiers to question God's ability, His Word, His Power, and His messengers. Bounds, and the others who stayed, assured the men that God could see them through any situation, even the siege of Vicksburg. "My grace is sufficient for thee: for my strength is made perfect in weakness" (2 Cor. 12:9).

On May 19, 1863, every man was in his place as the formal siege of Vicksburg began and the city became an isolated region filled with sniper and cannon fire. The constant noise of the cannons not only brought much physical damage and injury but gravely affected the emotions of both troops and civilians.

While in garrison at Vicksburg, Bounds received his commission orders from the Secretary of War of the Confederate States of America, which had been acted upon by Congress on May 13. It was Cockrell who swore Bounds in as captain of the Confederacy and as chaplain. Though some chaplains were volunteers or assigned by their denomination, many were officially commissioned by the Congress of the Confederacy to the position of chaplain. Very few received rank. One reason was the salary; another was to shield them from duties for which they would otherwise be responsible. But in case of capture, rank would place a chaplain in an officer's status and provide him more comfort and military courtesy. Rank also afforded the privilege of riding a horse, but Bounds never took advantage of this privilege.

While visiting the hospital, Bounds tried to call on his cousins Richard D. and Thaddeus only to find that they had been released and sent back to their units. However, it was brought to his attention that a Benjamin Bounds had been placed in the hospital. The first meeting of these first cousins divulged the fact that both were clergy in the Methodist Episcopal Church South. Much time was spent together praying and discussing the Holy Scriptures. While recovering, Benjamin was visited by yet another cousin, James Rufus Bounds, and the three Bounds men enjoyed a sweet time of fellowship, learning about one another and their families.

Days quickly became weeks in Vicksburg. Tragedy struck again and again. Grant used any means to break through the Confederate forces. On one occasion, 2,200 pounds of black powder exploded beneath the Third Louisiana Redan, creating a gaping crater. The defenders were stunned and found themselves buried under earth and debris. As the Union forces flooded the position, southern troops cried out in pain, suffering, and death.

Immediately the Missouri troops were thrust into the battle. For the next twenty-four hours furious hand-to-hand battle raged. Finally General Grant called for a withdrawal of his troops, and the fortification was reestablished.

This battle caused Bounds to reflect upon a spiritual principle taught in Ezekiel 22:30: "I sought for a man among them, that should make up the hedge, and stand in the gap before me for the land, and I should not destroy it: but I found none." Bounds realized how strategically General Pemberton had held the fighting group in reserve, so that whenever there was a breach in the line these well-disciplined, determined men could be thrust into the situation to protect the fortifications.

As it is in the battlefield of man, so it is in the spiritual battlefield. God is looking for men and women who will stand in the gap and make up the hedge to protect the nation from the wiles of satanic forces. It is an elite group, spiritually prepared and determined to do what God wants them to do that can step into any situation and bring spiritual stability and victory to the battle. As Bounds reflected on the battle, he realized the importance of this spiritual fact. In many of his later sermons, he would preach on this very theme. Bounds knew that it was the intercessors, those willing to pay with their life and give their life to intercede for others, who played the part of "standing in the hedge" for God's glory.

The siege began to have its effect as food, medicine, and morale became scarce. Only death, suffering, hunger, and despair abounded. Civilians were forced to hide in caves under the bluffs of the city as they tried to escape gunfire. The editor of the newspaper in Vicksburg so desired to keep the people informed with news both in Vicksburg and across the country that he continued to print it even when he ran out of paper. He ingeniously began printing on the blank side of wallpaper, and distributed the news among the troops and refugees in the caves right up until the day of surrender.

On July 1 the Union troops tried once again to penetrate the Louisiana Redan but met with failure. The casualty toll was heavy on the Confederate forces, the defenders being noticeably weaker. Food was in short supply and the main staple became bread made from field-pea meal. Occasionally the men ate mule meat.

As Bounds witnessed this terrible siege, he was overcome by his own helplessness. He worked endlessly to aid the victims of war and to point the hopeless and dying to the Savior. But he quickly realized his inadequacy and sought God afresh. Perhaps in Vicksburg, amid the misery and anguish, the weapon of prayer became Bounds' most valued possession and useful tool. "The effectual fervent prayer of a righteous man availeth much" (James 5:16).

On July 3, after a skimpy noon meal, the Missouri troops saw the flag of truce under a nearby shade tree. At about three o'clock General Grant met with General Pemberton, along with their staffs. Pemberton inquired of Grant the terms of surrender. Grant informed him that the terms were unconditional.

Early the next morning the Confederate troops marched from their trenches and laid down their arms. On Independence Day the city of Vicksburg was turned over to Union forces. The men in blue gave silent respect to the soldiers in gray, who had defended their charge for forty-seven days without allowing their line to be penetrated even once. The Confederate army had not lost a battle in Vicksburg, but they had lost the city to the siege.

Newly promoted Brigadier General Cockrell sent his report on the major role Missouri troops played in this battle, noting 559 casualties, 113 of those dead. He said the following of these courageous Missourians who gave their all to defend their convictions:

> This is a loss in killed and wounded of over one-third of the whole brigade, and shows that this brigade was almost continually, during the entire siege, exposed to enemy fire, and at no time during this eventful siege did these troops ever waver or fail to go to or occupy any point, regardless of its exposure, and frequently had to and did occupy points on the line so exposed that other troops, although on their own line, would give them up

for these troops to occupy. They endured all the dangers, fatigue, exposure, and weaknesses consequent on the insufficient rations, with the most commendable cheerfulness and soldierly bearing, willing to endure all things for the safety of the garrison, and desirous of holding out and fighting as long as there was a cartridge or a ration of mule or horse, and when the garrison capitulated, they felt, and were, disarmed, but in nowise whipped, conquered, or subjected. . . .

At the Stockade Redan, the Missouri troops both blue and gray had fought each other on the hallowed ground of Vicksburg. Missourians here again spilled their blood in a state other than Missouri. Today on that battlefield there stands a monument to the Missouri troops of both the North and the South. It is the only such monument found in the United States of America.

During this time the Confederate soldiers were considered prisoners of the Union army. They would be given paroles but could not take up arms. This would remain in effect until they were exchanged at prison camps located in various areas of the country. Prison exchange camps were places set aside for paroled soldiers to be located until man-for-man exchanges could be made between Confederate and Union forces. After the prison exchanges had taken place, the men were free to again take up arms. Chaplains also signed statements not to take up arms while paroled. They, too, were at liberty to rejoin forces when the prisoner exchanges had been completed. (This practice lasted only through the battle of Chickamauga.) Because most chaplains were considered noncombatants at this stage of the war, Bounds was never registered as a captured prisoner.

During the paroling of the men, the duties of the chaplains became lighter. One day a soldier in a Union uniform came calling for Bounds. It seems a cousin he knew of only slightly, Isaac I. Bounds, had come to seek assistance for his brother, Thomas M. Bounds. Thomas had served in the Thirty-Second Missouri Volunteer Infantry of the Union Army and had been wounded in Vicksburg. E. M. Bounds was given a release to attend his dying cousin. Boarding a Union hospital ship on the riverfront, he found his cousin from Scotland County, Missouri, close to death. After a brief conversation, Thomas was ushered into the presence of God. Chaplain Bounds escorted Isaac and the body of his brother and conducted services. (Thomas M. Bounds' body is interred in the Vicksburg National Cemetery.)

Several chaplains during this time had opportunity to return to Missouri. Bounds reminded them that he would be unable to return due to his banishment order. One of the chaplains who returned to Missouri was Bounds' dear friend Dr. William Caples, who agreed to take letters to the family. Caples fulfilled his promises to Bounds and then returned to his church in Glasgow, Missouri. But Caples was not yet finished with the war. Within the year, while standing in his own front yard, a cannon shot from a Confederate gun would take his life. This Confederate unit was firing a warning shot at the Union troops that were following them. But when the shot misfired, it struck Dr. Caples. The deadly blow was fired from a unit where Caples had served as chaplain.

By mid-July the prisoners had assembled. They would receive a parole that would allow them to travel to the prisoner exchange locations. Those who could walk were free to leave, and this group included Bounds. As he prepared to leave Vicksburg, he visited with his cousins still recovering from their wounds. Then, once again, Brother Bounds was on the move with the fire of the Holy Spirit in his being and a prayer on his lips: "Lord, direct my path."

7

The Battle for Atlanta

I hold—
That it becomes no man to nurse despair,
But in the teeth of clenched antagonisms
To follow up the worthiest till he die.

—Tennyson

The paroled Missouri troops, selected to be the first to leave Vicksburg, began marching to Edwards Station on the morning of July 11. The trek along the southern railroad was hot and humid and the 170 miles between Vicksburg and Enterprise, Mississippi, seemed to stretch before them in a dusty, sweltering steam bath.

The weary soldiers reached Enterprise twelve days later. Fortunately the men were able to travel by train from Enterprise to Meridian, Mississippi, where they were allowed a short furlough. Bounds took advantage of the respite and sought out the families of his cousins. He was surprised to learn that his cousin George W. Bounds had been in Vicksburg and also had returned to Mississippi that same day.

After a few days the men were on the road again. This time the destination was a parole camp that had been established at Demopolis, Alabama, where they would await prison exchange. It fell to Brig. Gen. Francis M.

Cockrell, as the only general from Missouri left on the eastern side of the Mississippi River, to reform the Missouri troops in Alabama into a fighting force. Many across the Confederacy were very impressed at how quickly and how easily he was able to accomplish this. The reorganization and training was so effective that in the early days of October, President Davis came to Demopolis for the specific purpose of reviewing the 7,000 Missouri troops gathered there. As he stood before these brave soldiers, he delivered the following message:

> I look with sadness on your reduced ranks and feel it is a high honor to be in the presence of such chivalrous soldiers. I have heard of your heroism on the bloody fields of the West and must express to you the high regard which I cherish for your privations and positive suffering in the cause of liberty. I thank you from the deepest recesses of my heart, from its very fiber, for your doubtless courage and untiring devotion to our common cause. Be assured that I express but the sentiments of our entire countrymen when I address you in the most fervent terms of gratitude, and I impress upon you that you have but to be true to the past and the memory of your ascended chief, yet to see the realization of your proudest desire for our country. May you look to the flag of our infant republic, its ensign of a great nation . . . among the nations' colors of the world. When this vision of joy is ours it will be due to your own brave hearts and stout arms. Again, I thank you.

In gratitude, the Missouri troops broke out in a regimental cheer, counting rapidly from one to nine, with each number increasing in volume and then holding on the number nine until it was a loud roar, as a mighty wind gushing across the countryside. Each man lifted and waved his hat, twirling it vigorously. President Davis turned his horse to ride away, and it was said on his cheeks were the tears of compassion, gratitude, and love.

As the men settled in, and autumn turned to winter, they moved back to Meridian to begin preparations for building houses to accommodate the troops. During this time they also built halls or chapels where they held services, which became very popular. Through the long winter days and nights, chess groups, debating clubs, and book report groups began to form. Later, after General Cockrell discovered gambling in some of the halls, all of the halls were ordered torched. Cockrell was a kind, considerate man, and his stalwart discipline led his men to respect and revere him. His cool leadership gave them reason to follow him unquestionably. His strong statement against gambling was well understood among the men, but the halls were never allowed to be rebuilt or relocated.

In the middle of winter, the Missouri Third was relocated to Greensboro, Alabama, just south of Demopolis. Dr. William May Wightman, President of the Southern University (a Methodist Episcopal Church South Institution) developed a strong friendship with Bounds. Because of their church affiliation and strong pietistic convictions they bonded in spirit and in service. Dr. Wightman invited Bounds to hold a meeting at the university chapel that led to a mighty outpouring of the grace of God. The fire of revival spread from Demopolis to Tuscaloosa, and pastors responded from faraway Selma and Mobile.

To hinder this mighty movement of God, Satan sent a diversion. The call came for troops to be sent to Mobile, Alabama, where a mutiny was about to erupt. On January 8, 1864, the Missouri troops boarded a train to travel the 120 miles south to put down the alleged mutiny. However, when they arrived nothing happened, and the Missouri troops returned on January 19 to Morton, Mississippi.

A month later, the Missouri troops were once again

moved to the Greensboro and Demopolis area. Local pastors, upon hearing of Bounds' return, tried to revive and restore the meetings in hopes that the movement of God would continue in the same manner. This did not happen, however, and Bounds was quick to warn that they should worship God himself, not seek after experience or manifestations.

The troops remained in this rich, lush valley in the heartland of the South until late spring. On March 8 the Missouri troops renewed their pledge to the Confederacy for "southern independence for forty years, or peace." Two weeks later the Confederate Congress in a joint resolution stated,

> It is resolved by the Confederate States of America that the thanks of Congress is extremely due, and is hereby tended to Brigadier General F. M. Cockrell and the officers and soldiers composing the 1st, 2nd, 3rd, 4th, 5th, and 6th regiments of the Missouri Infantry . . . all in the service of the Confederacy east of the Mississippi River, for the prompt renewal of their pledges of fidelity to the cause of Southern Independence for 40 years, unless independence and peace, without a curtailment of borders, shall be center secured.

At the same time, the Missouri troops were presented with a battle flag that was of the same configuration as the second national flag of the Confederacy. Called the "Stainless Banner," this white flag had a Union Jack in the upper left-hand corner. (This flag is now enshrined at Kennesaw National Battlefield in Georgia.) This was the first and only time this flag was given and permitted to be used as a battle flag during the entire Civil War. There was the fear that the corner of the flag would be concealed and the flag would be mistaken for the white flag of surrender.

In preparation for the coming campaign, the Missouri

troops were placed in the hands of Lt. Gen. Leonides Polk. It was during this time that Bounds started to develop a close spiritual and social friendship with General Polk, an American Episcopalian. Their friendship began when Bounds introduced General Polk to Frank S. Lyon, one of the leading Christian layman in the town of Demopolis. Lyon, a horse trainer, gave to General Polk a fine mount, named Jerry, and offered one to Brother Bounds to replace the "mule from Arkansas." Because of his rank as captain and chaplain, Bounds could have accepted this offer, but he turned it down to be able to identify himself with the common troops as he walked alongside them. The friendship between Bounds, Polk, and Lyon was fast and secure.

Early in May General Cockrell received orders to move to Montevallo, Alabama, to await transportation to Rome, Georgia. The Missouri troops were needed in Georgia as quickly as possible to try to disrupt General Sherman's march from Chattanooga toward Atlanta. With the Missouri troops scattered over six counties north of Tuscaloosa, Alabama, the feat that the Missouri troops performed in the following days had never been attempted and has not since been rivaled. Historically, much attention had been given to the fleet cavalry of Stonewall Jackson in Virginia for moving so far and so quickly, but the Missouri troops that May were acknowledged to have surpassed even those movements.

They moved from 117 miles north of Tuscaloosa to Montevallo, Alabama, where they traveled by train for sixty miles to Blue Mountain, Alabama. Then, in three days—in rain and on terrible roads—the troops marched seventy-five miles to reach Rome, Georgia. In Rome they acquired transportation by train for the fifteen miles to Kingston, then north to fight the battle of Resaca. In eleven days the Missouri Brigade moved two hundred and seventy-five miles, two hundred of them on foot. The last five to seven miles of their march, the men had to walk in a stooped position because they were under constant fire from the Union troops trying to block their movement.

The Missouri troops were quickly entrenched in their battle line. General Johnston set his troops in Resaca along a line from the Oostanaula River on the north, running south parallel with the Western Atlantic Railroad for three and one half miles. The Missouri troops, under command of General Cockrell, were at the south end close to the Conasauga River. They dug in well, looking across a small creek and open valley. On the western hillside, on the evening of May 13, the Seventeenth and Thirty-Second Missouri Union troops moved up to Camp Creek and took up positions on both sides of Lafayette Road.

Bounds took the opportunity, as they camped along the river, to speak of the Word of Living Water that ran through the valley of the shadow of death. He said that by the next day this water would be stained with the blood of man, but the blood of Jesus never leaves a stain, only a mark. And that the water of the creek would continue to run just as the hostility of man against man continued in their quest for selfish desires.

During the night, General Johnston, on advice of his field commanders, fell back behind the Etowah River. This did not deter Sherman from using the same tactics that Grant was using against Lee. Sherman used a flanking action to try to go around the troops and cut their supply line. Johnston did not fall for the trap and moved himself to throw Sherman off his plan. Johnston believed that the lives of his men should never be risked needlessly. Therefore, he never entered into a battle without the confidence that he could be victorious. This attitude stemmed from his experience at Gettysburg, when on the last day of battle thousands of lives were sacrificed needlessly because of inaccurate information, poor leadership, and poorly administered battle techniques. Johnston was dedicated to winning the war but desired to do so without useless sacrifice. Because he was outnumbered and outgunned by Sherman, Johnston used strategic movements rather than engaging in battles that he knew he would lose. Johnston patiently waited for the most favorable circumstances before facing Sherman's troops.

On May 20 it started to rain and for the next nineteen days it never ceased. This made life almost impossible. Without any hot food or dry clothing for the Union or Confederate forces, taking care of the wounded and sick became a major task. Still, the fighting continued, and many died at Pumpkin Vine Creek, Dallas, and New Hope Church.

General Johnston drew the army of Tennessee southward trying to establish a line that would be defensible without being flanked or encircled, jeopardizing the railroad and the supply line. This southerly withdrawal gave Bounds the opportunity to minister to many of the troops. When he arrived at the defense line on May 25, he found a small Methodist meetinghouse called New Hope Church. A stand was made here that would become notorious throughout the remainder of the Civil War, and trench warfare was forever changed from a defensive measure to a new level of maneuvering. Movement of troops from one location to another, as well as skirmishes within the trench lines themselves, became a new war tactic during this siege.

Bounds met Henry Lay, the Episcopal Bishop of Arkansas, who was ministering in the army of Georgia. He shared the stirring testimony of Gen. John Bell Hood. Two months earlier, on March 11, General Polk and General Hood had traveled from Resaca to Dalton for a staff meeting with General Johnston. General Hood was tied in his saddle with leather straps due to the loss of his leg in the battle of Chickamauga. While riding, Polk and Hood talked of the upcoming battles. Hood asked Polk if he would baptize him that night. So, at Johnston's headquarters, with artillery fire and minié balls flying over their heads, General Polk baptized General Hood in front of the officers and among the troops. Although Hood was so badly wounded he could not bow before Bishop-General Polk, he leaned on his crutches. His baptism was a tremendous testimony to the troops preparing for the terrible battles that lay ahead.

Before the battle at Resaca in early May, General Polk received a beautiful letter from General Johnston's wife, who had been told what had transpired between Generals Hood and Polk:

> You are never too much occupied, I well know, to pause to perform a good deed, and will, I am sure, even while leading your troops on to victory lead my soldier nearer to God. General Johnston has never been baptized, and it is the dearest wish of my heart that he would be and that you should perform the ceremony. It would be a great gratification to me. I have written to him on the subject and am sure he only waits your leisure. I rejoice that you are near him in these trying times. May God crown all your efforts with success and stay your life for your country and your friends.

Thus, on May 18, in the presence of General Hood and General Harding, General Johnston was baptized by Bishop-General Polk. "It was a deep, solemn scene, and what a passage for history!" Polk wrote to his wife. "God seemed to be drawing our hearts to Him. Our trust is not in chariots or horsemen, but in the living God. May He take and keep all our hearts until that day."

Cockrell and the Missouri troops were positioned on

the Dallas Road, four miles east of New Hope Church. After several days there, the Union forces started shifting eastward, and the Confederate troops adjusted to prevent the flanking operation. This required them to be moved to two low mountains just north of Marietta. One mountain was called Loft Mountain and the other Pine Mountain. Here, on a long battle line, the Confederate troops were stretched too thinly to defend themselves properly.

On June 14, while reinforcing their position, a great tragedy occurred. Generals Johnston, Harding, and Polk were observing the Federal lines. There in the distant trees, a cannon battery was being placed. General Sherman, who happened to ride by, instructed the soldiers to fire several rounds up the mountain toward the men standing there silhouetted and vulnerable. The first round landed close-by but without injury. The generals, now realizing the danger, quickly began to move. Two more rounds landed nearby, still with no incident of harm. General Polk was angling for a better view of the valley and the Federal guns that were firing. A cannon shot exploded near him and shrapnel tore through his chest, taking his life. "We are confident, I say, and willing rather to be absent from the body, and to be present with the Lord" (2 Cor. 5:8).

As General Polk lay on the ground, blood saturating his clothing, the pages of three identical tracts were stained in his pocket. They were written by Chaplain Quintard and entitled *Balm for the Weary and Wounded*. Each had been inscribed by General Polk for Generals Johnston, Harding, and Hood: "With the compliments of Lt. Gen. Leonides Polk, June 12, 1864." No doubt they were intended to be delivered that very morning. Upon receiving his copy, General Johnston, with tears streaming down his face, replied, "The autograph, and the noble blood that almost effaces it, makes it a souvenir truly precious, one which I shall cherish while the Almighty leaves me on earth."

Chaplains Bounds and Quintard quickly availed themselves to move with the body by train to the city of Marietta to await the arrival of Mrs. Polk and her daughters. After their arrival, Bounds hurried back to the troops, which had reformed at Kennesaw Mountain. With the civilians evacuating the area, getting back to the troops was difficult. Finally he arrived at a tiny spur off Kennesaw Mountain, called Pigeon Hill, where the Missouri troops were well entrenched in the dense brush.

The battle of Kennesaw Mountain began on June 27. With rain coming in torrents and lightning striking all around them, the Missouri men held their line for four and one half hours. The rain stopped as the battle ended, and the sun came shining forth as if a new day approached. This battle was devastating to Bounds, as forty-one of his men died that day. It was even more costly to General Sherman, who suffered approximately two thousand casualties and a significant setback.

During this battle, Bounds was given a unique opportunity. Two men, diametrically opposed to each other spiritually, were seriously wounded. He hurried to the aid of his wounded friend and leader, Gen. Francis Cockrell. As he ministered to Cockrell, General Hickey was hit in the shoulder and was quite near death. Bounds worked with both men, assuring Cockrell of God's loving watch-care, while trying to point Hickey, a man angry and running from God, to salvation in Christ. Bounds escorted both men from the battlefield to Davis Hospital in Marietta, and quickly returned to the troops. Here again, the Missouri troops from the Confederacy had fought the Missouri troops of the Union.

As the battle for Atlanta raged, Bounds stayed with the wounded until late evening, when he made his way through to the trenches to hand out tracts and read the

Word of God to the men who would be facing battle again in the morning. Often he would write letters home for the soldiers who could not read or write. He would almost always bring word of the condition of their wounded comrades. And, as often as was permitted, he would deliver sweet cakes, cold biscuits, honey or sorghum, and the many other treats the civilians sent to encourage the young men fighting far from home.

Sorrow and despair hung over the battlefield like a thick fog; it seemed that the Spirit of God was quiet and unmoving. But even during these most distressful times, God was ever watching his children and using even the harm that men inflict on one another for the glory of Jesus Christ. "When my spirit was overwhelmed within me, then thou knewest my path" (Ps. 142:3).

As Bounds struggled over the battlefield day after day, the earth covered with splintered pines and the mangled bodies of men, his heart was heavily burdened. Where were the souls of the men whose bodies lay waiting to be returned to the earth from which they'd come? Were they with the Savior, now in perfect peace? Or were they in everlasting judgment, forever separated from God almighty in eternal torment? The sight drove him to his knees and to the continued labor of God in the sharing of the Gospel with as many men as he could. "Let him know, that he which converteth the sinner from the error of his way shall save a soul from death, and shall hide a multitude of sins" (James 5:20).

The army chaplains tried to assist the local pastors and civilians during the bombardment of Atlanta, and often used the churches to worship together. Samuel Pierce Richards shared the account of such a meeting. He wrote, "I listened to a sermon at the Methodist church, by Rev. Atticus Haygood, and the next night Rev. Edward Bounds brought a sermon."

On July 17 orders were given by President Jefferson

Davis, changing command of the Confederate troops in Atlanta from Gen. Joseph E. Johnston to Gen. John B. Hood. The troops were devastated at the news. "Old Joe" had brought them from Chattanooga to Atlanta, at a far greater cost to the enemy than to themselves. They had great confidence in General Johnston and of success in Atlanta. When the news that General Hood was now in command reached the troops, a "universal gloom seemed cast over the army." Bearded men wept, and many threw aside their arms and deserted. The once high morale was now at an all time low.

The army of Tennessee had little confidence in General Hood, and many officers felt the same. This caused instability throughout the ranks, as orders that were once followed without question were now being scrutinized. Even the Union army believed the decision would benefit them greatly, and General Sherman said, "At this critical moment, the Confederate government has rendered us a most valuable service."

The purely political decision had been made in the back rooms of Richmond. And Hood proved to be a fatal selection for the defending of Atlanta. Those advising President Davis had personal gain in mind, or favored personalities, but no regard for the benefit of the cause or for those who might suffer. They only saw their chance to climb the ladder of political acclaim.

This experience impacted Bounds in a mighty way. He was emphatic throughout the remainder of his ministry that self-serving ambition is devastating to the welfare of men; that it originated with Satan himself, and is the chief cause of man's downfall. "Only by pride cometh contention: but with the well advised is wisdom. Wealth gotten by vanity shall be diminished: but he that gathereth by labour shall increase" (Prov. 13:10–11).

Another truth that Bounds gained from this ordeal was that decisions made behind closed doors are often made without integrity. Jesus never made any decision that was not public. "Jesus answered him, 'I spake openly to the world; I ever taught in the synagogue, and in the temple, whither the Jews always resort; and in secret have I said nothing' " (John 18:20). The Bible itself is proof that God works publicly. Bounds was convinced that preachers' only secret work should be in their prayer closets; that their lives should be open to examination. "Moreover he must have a good report of them which are without; lest he fall into reproach and the snare of the devil" (1 Tim. 3:7).

The constant shelling and fighting began to take its toll on the city of Atlanta. Supplies were low, and the men were tired of fighting for months without victory. Without a trusted leader, the Confederate troops had little hope of any change. These conditions made the Word of God the only security the men could embrace. The movement of God in Dalton the previous winter had enabled the men to see some of their comrades die with hope and confidence in God. Now, in what seemed a hopeless situation, the men sought the One who could bring peace to their souls. A Union soldier wrote,

> On duty after dark, the Sixth Iowa heard services carried on late into the night; shouting and singing could be distinctly heard in the Confederate lines. A Missouri chaplain [probably E. M. Bounds] wanted soldiers to be Christians, as they would not fear the consequences after death as others do.

The Union troops were often reported to stop their shelling in the evening so they could hear the hymns of worship coming from the rebel troops, many times joining in the songs of praise with their enemy and calling requests of prayer across Confederate lines.

The revival continued throughout the siege of Atlanta. Bounds again found himself in the trenches more than in the city. Just south of the city, in a little white Methodist church that stood among the great oak trees, mourners of the casualties did not cease to pray. Without the leadership of man, they had the leadership of God, and the people wept and prayed at the altar continuously for weeks. "Men ought always to pray, and not to faint" (Luke 18:1).

Just as Jesus wept for Jerusalem, the citizens of Atlanta in the Owl Rock Methodist Church wept for the city as never before or since. Upon invitation of the pastor, Bounds held meetings in the church. He called for the Christians to sing the songs of Zion for God's glory, while he asked those not in the family of God to remain silent and listen to the praises of the Creator. Then, standing straight as an arrow taut in a bow, Bounds would go straight to the Cross of Calvary. He often preached regarding hell, sin, and eternal death; issues that were critical to the men who heard them. With his uniform buttoned to the neck, his light brown hair neatly combed, and his beard trimmed, Bounds implored the men to turn to Jesus. His concern for souls was so real that tears streamed down his face as he spoke.

On August 8 Bounds was summoned to battalion headquarters. There he was brought before his old friend and commander, General Cockrell, who had returned to battle as soon as his wounds had healed. Cockrell requested that Bounds lead the group in prayer as they rejoiced in the return of their leader.

As the siege continued, the efforts of ministry and evangelism also continued. A report from Rev. S. M. Cherry, agent for the Soldier's Tract Association of the Methodist Episcopal Church South in the army of Tennessee, gave clear testimony of the work performed:

Again, at four in the afternoon, I preached for Cockrell's Missouri Brigade, where a fine revival was in progress: above one hundred of those gallant Missourians, far away from their homes, have sought and secured a title to a home in the many mansioned house of our Father in heaven. Among the number, a noble young officer of fine intellect joined the church one day, and was killed on the post of duty the day following: August 31, 1864.

On September 1 the final blow came. With battles all about the city, there was constant bombardment of cannon fire. With defeat in the battle of Jonesboro and the destruction of the last railroad that could deliver supplies, Hood ordered the evacuation of the city of Atlanta. Supplies in army warehouses were opened to the residents of the city, and all that was not taken was burned. The ammunition train was exploded, and the troops began to withdraw. Sherman occupied Atlanta the next day.

The Missouri brigade was the last of the troops to leave the city. Surrendering the city was completely against their Missouri culture. They made up the rear guard and fought their way out. They traveled down the old McDonough Road until they reached Lovejoy Station, where they held the Union forces long enough for the army to regroup. They held this position through the month of September.

On September 25 President Jefferson Davis addressed the Confederate troops. He tried to justify the change of command from General Johnston to General Hood by questioning General Johnston's devotion to the cause. Such talk was not well received, and Bounds was greatly troubled that Johnston was so accused without opportunity to defend himself.

8

Massacre at Franklin

"Good prayers," says an old divine, "never come weeping home. I am sure I shall receive either what I ask, or what I should ask. Prayer pulls the rope below, and the great bell rings above in the ears of God. Some scarcely stir the bell, for they pray so languidly; others give but an occasional pull at the rope; but he who wins with heaven is the man who grasps the rope boldly and pulls continuously with all his might."

That is the best kind of bell ringing—ringing the bells of heaven—making a sensation in the world celestial, and pulling the power down upon the world terrestrial. Reader, do you know how to handle the bell rope, to pull it vigorously and constantly? We know some that do. Hell trembles when they seize the rope.

—E. M. Bounds
(First published in *The Christian Standard*)

With the embers of Atlanta smoking behind them, the fire in the Confederate army was flickering. Desertion and defection became a daily problem. Soldiers felt that the politicians had sold them out, using their blood as a bartering chip. Even those who remained were angry at the political leaders for their self-seeking motives.

This attitude gave Bounds and the other chaplains

quite a challenge as they tried to encourage the weary men. Bounds' sermons often carried the theme "the last shall be first." He reminded the soldiers that the Word of God teaches that those seeking power, prestige, wealth, control, and popularity will be last in the kingdom of God. "But many that are first shall be last; and the last shall be first" (Matt. 19:30).

On October 1 Hood's men began to move. Going from Palmetto to Dark Corner, Flat Hill Church, and Carley's House, the men welcomed the cooler temperatures that came with the changing seasons. The Missouri troops were sent to help in the battle of Altoona, but defeat came quickly. Two weeks later all of Hood's men found themselves back in Dalton, Georgia.

Hood wanted to draw Sherman out of Georgia. So on October 17 he moved his men, planning to go northwest through Tennessee and toward Ohio. Sherman pursued Hood only for a few days and then he turned back toward Atlanta to begin his march to the sea.

Hood continued his quest. His army camped at the small river town of Tuscumbia, Alabama, waiting for transport across the Tennessee River. When at last they crossed the river, miserable cold weather met the men head on. Winter arrived earlier than the local people could ever remember. The rain soon mixed with sleet and snow, and the poorly clad troops were distressed. Not only were jackets and blankets scarce, many men were even without shoes. Some became unable to move as the blood from their feet froze to the icy ground.

As Hood continued north, the Union army, led by Gen. John Schofield, was on the move just south of them. Schofield was under orders to reinforce the garrison at Nashville. Hood wanted to stop Schofield before he reached Nashville.

At the small town of Spring Hill, Hood succeeded in cutting Schofield off from his objective. But on the night of November 29, in a brazen show of daring, Schofield and his men silently marched right through the town as the rebel army slept in exhaustion. When Hood realized what had happened, he was furious. He threw caution and reason to the wind, and started in pursuit of the Federal troops.

The next day, in the little town of Franklin, Tennessee, the two armies came together. Franklin was very supportive of the Confederate army. The town had been occupied by the Union army for a long time, and they were eager for the rebels to take the town back, even if it meant their own sons would be in the thick of the fighting.

The sun hid its face behind a dark winter cloud, unwilling to look upon the dismal scene that was to unfold on the flat cotton fields of Tennessee. The 620 butternut-clad Missouri men stood with bayonets fixed upon their weapons. Their eyes were set on the enemy that stood before them.

At four o'clock in the afternoon the banners unfurled. The band switched from the "Bonnie Blue Flag" to "Dixie." A ferocious rebel yell went up, and the 900 yards that stood between the two armies was quickly washed in the blood of those gallant men. The battle raged at Franklin between the Big Harpeth River and the Carter Creek Pike. There in the "valley of no return," the Missouri Brigade lost 68 percent of its fighting force.

The fighting was so furious in Franklin that all human restraint was gone. When their weapons were lost, the soldiers used whatever they could find to fight their enemy. And when nothing was available, they used their bare fists, even resorting to biting and gnashing with their teeth. "Their feet run to evil, and they make haste to shed innocent blood: their thoughts are thoughts of iniquity; wasting and destruction are in their paths" (Isa. 59:7).

Though Bounds had been asked to remain at the rear with the chaplains and medical personnel, he was found in the midst of the fighting trying to help the wounded and dying. As the troops went up the earthworks at Franklin Pike, General Cockrell was shot from his mount. Bounds had started after his friend, when a searing pain creased his forehead. He had received the blow of a Union saber. The cut was shallow but it bled profusely. When Bounds regained his senses, he found Cockrell and Captain Hickey together. Both men were seriously wounded; particularly Hickey, who had been hit three times, his right leg completely severed. Bounds enlisted the help of some men nearby and got the two officers off the battlefield before the Union troops came back to reclaim their positions.

The already cold temperatures continued to drop and sleet began to fall. Soon the field was covered with ice, and the dead and dying lay silently, alone in the winter darkness.

The defeat at Franklin was devastating for the Confederacy. As the Union army marched on to Nashville, the little town of Franklin took in the 4,000 wounded men left behind. These poor people had few resources, but they poured out their hearts and opened their homes and public buildings to the men who were suffering— both in the blue and the gray.

The day following the battle was a day of burial. The Federal troops, left where they had fallen, were covered with dirt from the earthworks. This act would help with identification later on. The Confederate troops were placed shoulder to shoulder, a piece of blanket over their faces, in a trench two feet deep. Small boards, with the known names written on them, served as markers. Brother Bounds tried to keep track of where the men from Missouri were laid. As he did so, he found that his brigade had lost a higher percentage than any other.

Cockrell and Hickey were both taken to a little Methodist church building to recuperate. During one of Bounds' visits with Hickey, he asked the officer if he would like some Scripture read and a prayer said. Hickey answered, "No, no, get me some beer or whiskey, tell me some anecdotes, and I'll pull through."

Bounds was greatly disappointed that a man in his condition would reject God for the second time. But rather than condemn him, he prayed that God would continue to deal with this rebellious soldier. (History proved Bounds a faithful witness. When the two men met again after the war, it was discovered that Hickey had embraced the loving God who had sought him for so long. Now a changed man, Hickey thanked Dr. Wooldridge for his medical care and Mrs. Carter, who had opened her Franklin home to the recovering Confederate soldier. Hickey later returned to Columbia, Missouri, where he married a beautiful young woman. He served faithfully in his Methodist church as a laypreacher.)

The town of Franklin has had volumes written about the heroic sacrifices made during the Civil War. The generosity and compassion of the citizens stood in direct contrast to the inhumane and brutal fighting that erupted in the city. As Bounds visited the wounded troops, he was asked to visit those Union troops housed in the Presbyterian church. There he discovered—as in Vicksburg and Kennesaw—Missouri troops had fought against each other. Here he met men he knew, or men whose families he knew, and he tried to give comfort and encouragement. But his heart was grieved that the bodies of Missouri men would lie in the ground of Tennessee, put there by other Missouri men.

What remained of the army of Tennessee moved on to Nashville, and in the next eighteen days a futile battle raged that rendered Hood's army totally ineffective. Col. Peter F. Flournoy, a boyhood friend of Bounds, was or-

dered to return with his men south of Nashville and secure a way of escape. Flournoy brought the troops back
through Franklin.

Bounds was at Carter House with General Cockrell,
in Franklin, when the messenger arrived with news of
Hood's defeat in Nashville. Hood was in full retreat, so
General Cockrell and the men recovered enough from
their wounds to travel had to leave Franklin with the brigade.

Bounds had to make a difficult decision. There were
still many wounded men, some at the point of death, in
Franklin. Because Bounds' heart was always with the
men who had the greatest need, when his brigade left
Franklin, he remained. He felt the presence of clergy
would ensure better treatment for the injured.

As Hood's army went south by train, the Union troops
invaded Franklin from the north. On December 17, 1864,
Bounds and the wounded men who remained in the city
were classified as captured. Many of them were loaded
onto flatbed railroad cars and sent to Nashville as prisoners. Most would never reach their destination; many
had no blankets or coats and would die of the cold, others
would die of their wounds without medical treatment.
Schofield insisted this operation be handled very quickly
because the Federals needed the trains to continue their
pursuit of General Hood. Once again, Bounds was allowed to remain in Franklin.

As he ministered to the needs of those around him, he
found a civilian population in want also. The war had put
an end to most regular church meetings, and the spiritual lives of the people lacked nourishment. He began to
meet for prayer with the men of the little white Methodist church on the corner of South and Church Streets.
Before long, Bounds was holding Bible studies in the
homes of the faithful in an effort to help the people find
their way into the arms of the loving Father.

He remained in Franklin until the early days of March, when all the wounded were sufficiently recovered to travel to Nashville. Upon their arrival, Bounds was placed in stockade on the public square. Policy had been changed during the war. Many chaplains had taken up arms against the Union, and the exemption of capture had been lifted under orders of General Grant.

As hope for the South's victory began to die, General Grant's plan to cut all supply lines from the South began to come together and take its toll. On March 17 Bounds gave the oath of allegiance to the United States of America before Col. J. G. Parkhurst, provost marshal of Nashville. On April 9, 1865, Robert E. Lee surrendered to Ulysses S. Grant at Appomattox Court House, Virginia. This, however, did not secure the release of Bounds, for his banishment from Missouri was in effect as long as there were hostilities in the nation.

At this point, Bounds and a few others were taken to the Tennessee State Penitentiary at the corner of Spring and Cedar Streets. News of Lee's surrender did not travel quickly. Johnston surrendered to Sherman on April 26; General Robert Taylor surrendered the Confederate forces of Mississippi, Missouri, and Alabama on May 4; and General Edward Kirby-Smith surrendered the last Confederate army still in the field on May 26 in Shreveport, Louisiana. On June 28, 1865, Bounds once again pledged his allegiance to the United States of America before Edward R. Campbell, Commissioner of the Circuit Court. Released at last, Bounds gave his word not to return to Missouri, as long as there were still skirmishes between forces or stragglers who had not heard that the fight to preserve the American Union had finally ended.

9

Return to Franklin

Ye different sects, who all declare,
"Lo, here is Christ!" or "Christ is there!"
Your stronger proofs divinely give,
And show me where the Christians live.
Your claim, alas! ye cannot prove;
Ye want the genuine mark of love:
Thou only, Lord, thine own canst show;
For sure thou hast a Church below.
Join every soul that looks to thee
In bonds of perfect charity;
Now, Lord, the glorious fullness give
And All in all forever live!

—Charles Wesley

E. M. Bounds walked out of the Tennessee Penitentiary a free man, but he was in dire need of physical restoration. He was almost thirty years of age, which was quite old for a Civil War veteran, and four years amid disease and infection and the lack of proper nutrition had taken its toll. The people of Franklin invited him back to the small Methodist church where Bounds had served so faithfully. Remembering with compassion the loving people of Franklin and their hunger for God almighty, Bounds accepted the invitation.

As the task of reconstruction began, Franklin was

71

still occupied by Union forces and operating under martial law, causing the bitterness of defeat to grow as many carpetbaggers took advantage of the poverty-stricken southerners. As Bounds sought to bridge every gap with the love of God, he was often misunderstood. His quiet demeanor and loving ways, however, soon melted the resentment some harbored as they considered the Savior that Bounds so consistently preached. "My little children, let us not love in word, neither in tongue; but in deed and in truth" (1 John 3:18).

Bounds' personal witness quickly caught the attention of Colonel Opedyke of the 125th Ohio Volunteer Infantry. Opedyke could not understand the compassion this preacher, still wearing his gray uniform, had for the soldiers in blue. He saw that the concern Bounds had for the souls of his men was far more effective in reaching them spiritually than anything he had ever seen, even among their own chaplains. As his respect for Bounds grew, Opedyke moved his troops out of the church and off of the church grounds they had occupied since March of 1862.

Bounds was without any financial support during most of the year, but the people found him dependable and undemanding and they were quite willing to share with their pastor whatever they had. Bounds suffered along with his people, grieving for their losses and enduring the change. This behavior was quite different from many preachers who were out to only better themselves. People discovered Bounds lived what he preached.

He believed wholeheartedly that a man's life must give credence to his speech lest it harden the heart of the observer. He was careful not to allow his intense desire for winning souls to deter the moving of the Holy Spirit, and he tried to be ever mindful of the leading of God in speaking to men.

As he went about serving the people of Franklin, he would often walk out to the battlefield, reliving those terrible days when the screams of the wounded and dying pierced the air. As he made these walks, he began to notice that many of the small boards marking the grave sites were missing, broken, or the writing had become obscured. He began to be burdened about these men having a proper burial ground.

Bounds was able to collaborate with the McGavock family, who lived only a mile or so out of town and close to the river, to set aside a plot of ground adjacent to their family cemetery for the burial of the men killed in the battle of Franklin. And so it was arranged that on a gentle sloping hill facing the battlefield, nestled in a tranquil spot amid thickets of cedar and mulberry trees, the men would be properly buried.

John D. Miller, a contruction company owner, accepted the gruesome responsibility of actually moving the bodies. He built the caskets and then secured someone to perform the interments. As news of the plan spread, money began to come in to finance the project. Then, as the warm winds of March began to thaw the frozen ground, Carnton Cemetery (the only exclusively Confederate cemetery in the nation) was plotted out, with each man placed according to the state in which he served.

Bounds felt this effort was truly directed by God. Often he would stand on the hallowed ground that entombed his fellow soldiers, and tears would stream down his face as his lips moved with prayers for their grieving families.

Finally, after many months of labor, the fence around the plot was secured and a blanket of green sod covered the resting place of 1,481 Confederate soldiers.

As the Union occupation continued, hatred grew in the hearts of the residents. Bounds patiently, lovingly, yet firmly preached the truth that hatred could not continue in the heart of a loving child of the heavenly Father.

"If I regard iniquity in my heart, the Lord will not hear me" (Ps. 66:18).

The Tennessee Conference was convened in Nashville, and one of the orders of business was to present Brother Edward McKendree Bounds the office of elder. This was great news and very encouraging to the flock in Franklin. There was much thanksgiving, and in recognition of their pastor, a dinner on the grounds was called. The entire community complied. The churches in the area began to talk of the old camp meetings that brought such tremendous spiritual growth, but decided to wait another year when they felt they could better support such an event.

This drove the Thursday night prayer band deeper into communion with God as they desperately prayed for revival. Then, after fifteen long months, God opened the heavens and the fire of revival came to the little church in Franklin. "Know therefore that the Lord thy God, he is God, the faithful God, which keepeth covenant and mercy with them that love him and keep his commandments to a thousand generations" (Deut. 7:9).

Here in this small town, where four years of Civil War had been suffered, God sent the consuming fire of revival for empowering and cleansing. It came with no announcement or warning. There was no plan, and the pastor had not sent for an evangelist to come and help him. But the revival continued for weeks, and the town and region were remarkably impacted. The conversation each day regarded those who had responded to God's call the night before. At the conclusion of the meeting, 150 people had made public confessions of their newfound faith in God.

Among the converts was a young boy by the name of B. F. Haynes, whose grandfather was also a pastor and strong leader in Franklin. His name was Rev. Mark L. Andrews. But it was Bounds who had the greatest influence on the young boy who would follow his grandfather into the ministry. Haynes would later become a noted preacher, the president of Asbury College in Wilmore, Kentucky, editor, and author. Haynes spoke of Bounds' influence in this manner:

> His preaching profoundly impressed me, his prayers linger until today, as one of the holiest and sweetest memories of my life. His reading of hymns was simply inimitable. Nothing was sweeter, more tender, or more enrapturing to my young heart and mind than the impressive, unctuous reading of the old Wesleyan hymns by this young pastor. I never hear these hymns today or think of them that the scene is not reenacted of the little hazel-eyed, black-haired pastor with a voice of divine love standing in the pulpit of the old Methodist church, reading one of these matchless hymns in a spirit, tone, and manner that simply poured life, hope, peace, and holy longings into my boyish heart.

The work in Franklin continued to prosper. Bounds poured his life into those around him. He was never afraid to try something different. He even took the radical (for that day) step of placing announcements of church services in the local newspaper.

Many in the community came out to visit this church that "plowed new ground," and the church greatly impacted the community as it grew and prospered. The community responded with a gesture that was most gracious and charitable. In April 1868 a triangular plot of ground at the corner of South Fifth and Church Streets was presented to the church by the Chancery Court of the county.

Bounds began to prepare to build the greatly needed new church. The committees, legal needs, funding drive, and builder had been secured when the church received word that a new pastor, Rev. R. K. Hargrove, had been assigned to Franklin. The news was not well received by the people of Franklin, for they loved E. M. Bounds. But Bounds embraced the change with expectancy as a new opportunity of service to the Lord and His church.

10

Ministry in Selma and Eufaula

Be not afraid to pray—to pray is right.
Pray, if thou canst, with hope; but ever pray,
Though hope be weak, or sick with long delay;
Pray in the darkness, if there be no light.
Far is the time, remote from human sight,
When war and discord on the earth shall cease;
Yet every prayer for universal peace
Avails the blessed time to expedite,
Whate'er is good to wish ask that of Heaven,
Though it be what thou canst not hope to see:
Pray to be perfect, though material leaven
Forbid the spirit so on earth to be;
But if for any wish thou darest not pray,
Then pray to God to cast that wish away.

—Coleridge

Bounds, always eager to be about his Father's business, gathered his few belongings and boarded a train for Selma, Alabama, in the Tuscaloosa District. By January 1869 he was back at the Church Street Methodist Church where revival had broken out in 1863. Many of the members remembered Bounds and received him with great excitement and anticipation.

There was a different look about the city since Bounds had last seen it. The war had taken a great toll, and many of the homes and businesses were in ruins. The area near the Alabama River was particularly devastated. Often Bounds would walk down to the riverfront and grieve over the sight of those living in such extreme poverty and need. Among the rubble of the old Confederate Naval Foundry lived families—many of whom were freed slaves with no idea how to obtain employment. Bounds brought the needs of these people before the members of his congregation and they set about to do what they could to help. "He that hath pity upon the poor lendeth unto the Lord; and that which he hath given will he pay him again" (Prov. 19:17).

Soon the Federal government sent their political appointees into Selma to address the needs of those living in such distress. These government workers, rather than enlisting the help of the churches already involved, ridiculed and excluded them. Brother Bounds and his parishioners, many of whom were educators and businessmen, tried to protest, but the political forces called in the courts, and the church had to withdraw their help.

Bounds faithfully served the people of Selma for about three years before receiving word of a transfer. As the leaves on the trees turned crimson and gold, he looked forward to his new assignment.

In the fall of 1871, at the age of thirty-six, Edward McKendree Bounds gathered his possessions and moved to Eufaula, Alabama, to become the pastor of the First Methodist Episcopal Church South. He wasn't there long before he was confronted by the great problems that beset this city located on the banks of the Chattahoochee River. The community was in upheaval. The turmoil of restoration and reconstruction had brought about a destructive political situation that was completely ineffective. The town had been torn apart socially; the police were incapable of keeping the peace; and murder, assault, and robbery were daily occurrences. That the hatred in this town had all but destroyed the fellowship and effectiveness of the local church was evidenced by the fact that not one soul had been converted in over two years. "Being filled with all unrighteousness, fornication, wickedness, covetousness, maliciousness; full of envy, murder, debate, deceit, malignity; whisperers, backbiters, haters of God, despiteful, proud, boasters, inventors of evil things, disobedient to parents, without understanding, covenantbreakers, without natural affection, implacable, unmerciful . . ." (Rom. 1:29–32).

Bounds knew more than ever before that his own pious life-style should be above reproach so that God might witness to others through him. He felt people would either understand and respond to the commitment, sacrifice, and obedience to God or they would move out of the church fellowship. Though Bounds prayed that all would accept God's authority, he was aware that God must occasionally prune away the dead branches in order for the church to grow and be an effective witness for Jesus Christ. "Every branch in me that beareth not fruit he taketh away: and every branch that beareth fruit, he purgeth it, that it may bring forth more fruit" (John 15:2). Bounds' work at the church required much time and prayer.

As spring arrived in this rural area, the blooming trees, azaleas, and flower gardens gave the impression that the town was laced with flowers. The breeze carried the sweet fragrance to every valley crevice, grassy dale, and mountaintop, making the world seem sweet and beautiful. But the streets told a different story. Crime continued to rise and racial tensions were to the point of bloodshed. One of the major annoyances was the local newspaper, so Bounds challenged the *Eufaula Times* to allow him to place an editorial column in the paper.

The *Times* agreed and Bounds began to write. The needs of the community were addressed without calling names and pointing fingers. Through his column, Bounds was able to confront problems intelligently, ethically, and without malice. He was always clear and to the point and focused on the disgrace of such social problems. In less than one month, Bounds' column was running in the *Barbour County Weekly*, and by year's end, papers across Georgia and Alabama ran his articles.

Around February of 1872, Bounds' name was presented to the Education Committee of the Alabama Conference, and he was elected to the Board of Trustees of Tuskagee Female College. While Bounds attended his first board meeting, the pastor of La Place Methodist Church asked him to stay and have a meeting with his congregation. He agreed to stay the remaining three days of the week.

By Friday night, the little clapboard building could not hold the crowds. The road to the church was blocked by wagons and buggies, an overflow of the church parking lot. Soon the crowd was so overwhelming that the meeting had to move out of the church building and convene beneath the trees. Then the problem was mosquitoes and gnats, and they moved the meeting to the First Church, two blocks from the college in Tuskagee.

God moved mightily and the meeting lasted for two weeks. Finally, with his other responsibilities beckoning, Bounds announced that he must return home to Eufaula. Many of the people were saddened at the news and feared the moving of God would leave with Bounds. However, he assured the people, "If it is of God, it will last, for God will abide in His meeting. If it is *not* of God, it should end, and it will." But the meeting did not end, and three weeks later every church in the region was still in meeting. This affirmed Bounds' conviction that God was not confined to one man. When God sends revival, all who are obedient and filled with the Holy Spirit can be instruments of His power.

While the Spirit of God was moving in revival in Tuskagee, it was not evident in Bounds' home parish. Hatred was at the forefront in Eufaula, and though financial prosperity had started to expand the community, peace among the people was still lacking.

On one occasion, racial conflict erupted in an armed confrontation. Bounds ended up in the middle of the crowd trying to hold both sides at bay. His courage, truth, and respect for all people, both white and black, held the people apart, yet many in the crowd continued to encourage a fight. The black man who looked after Bounds placed himself in harm's way and physically forced Bounds out of the conflict.

Early in the summer, Bounds was called to conduct a funeral for one of the local families. While at the cemetery, he looked up to see "the most beautiful woman in all the world." After the service, he quickly but tactfully sought information regarding this most enchanting young lady. He was told she was the daughter of his friend Dr. A. W. Barnett, and had been away visiting her cousins in Washington, Georgia, for several months. Her name was Emma Elizabeth Barnett. From that time forward, Bounds kept a close notice of Miss Barnett.

Personal sorrow arrived with a telegram on July 26, telling Bounds of his sister's death. The telegram from his mother asked, "Can you come?" He was on the next train home.

This was Bounds' first trip back to Missouri since his banishment and his emotions were erratic. When he arrived in St. Louis, the train made a stop at Jefferson Barracks, the spot where he had been placed on a steamship to carry him out of the state. Now he was coming back, not in a uniform of Confederate gray, but with the Word of God in his heart to share with his grieving family. It was a bittersweet reunion.

After the funeral, Bounds had time to visit with Gen. Sterling Price, who had returned to his hometown after the Civil War. The two had not seen each other since 1863. Eventually it was time to return home, but this time Bounds left Missouri out of responsibility to others, not by order of banishment.

On his return to Eufaula, Bounds really upset the status quo. With great personal rejoicing, on August 29, Bounds performed the wedding ceremony of Mr. Washington Poison and Miss Mary Sayers. The community was astonished that the pastor of the Methodist Episcopal Church South would perform the wedding of two Negroes. But Washington was a dear man who had served Bounds very diligently. And although it was not socially acceptable, Bounds felt it was scripturally and spiritually proper to honor this man and his bride by marrying them.

As the Spirit of God moved in Bounds' church, the little white-frame building soon became too small for its congregation. The building was only forty by sixty feet, with plain furniture, oiled pine floors, straight-back pews, a high pulpit, a wood-burning stove, and candle lighting. The church decided a larger and more modern facility was needed to provide better opportunity for reaching the community, and the decision was made to relocate.

While the church building was in progress, Bounds moved the worship services to Hart Hall. The church continued to grow, even though they did not have a "church house." During that time, Brother Bounds held a "protracted meeting." By the end of the meeting in June, forty-seven people had "connected themselves" with the church.

The *Tri-Weekly* newspaper placed an accounting of the church building as a main news article. The new church building would have the tallest steeple in the South; it was noted to be twenty-two feet higher than the steeple on the First Baptist Church. Another article pointed out, "We are informed that it is the intention of both the pastor and the members not to have outstanding debts when the time for its dedication arrives, which we trust will be imitated in the future in erecting houses of worship. . . ." The secular news noted the high standards the church embraced for itself under the pastor's convictions. It was Bounds' belief that no one should dedicate anything to God unless the church had total possession of the item. He believed a church or Christian could not dedicate to God the possessions of the world.

While all the notice of the community was on the construction of the church building, Bounds continued to write articles for the *Tri-Weekly* regarding his conviction of the need for pastors to use evangelists for their evangelistic meetings. A strong element in the churches across America felt pastors should conduct all of the meetings of the church. The proponents of this movement felt vocational evangelists would strip the churches of their finances and develop a cultic following. They feared the evangelist would destroy or compete with the work of the pastor. Bounds stood on the Bible teaching of a God-given call to evangelism and he began writing to that effect. His articles appeared in newspapers across the nation supporting the movement of evangelism and the involvement of the vocational evangelist. His declarations led to a close friendship with evangelist Sam Jones. "And he gave some, apostles; and some, prophets; and some, evangelists; and some, pastors and teachers" (Eph. 4:11).

After twelve months of building, the church was dedicated by Bishop John. C. Keener and E. M. Bounds on April 4, 1875. Bounds was elated at the dedication of the building, but what pleased him most was to evaluate his ministry during the construction period. When he arrived at the church, there were seventy-two adult members and 180 children and adults involved in Bible study and ministry. In less than four years, when the building was dedicated, the church had 247 adult members who were actively involved in the church and 280 adults and children involved in the Bible study program.

Later that fall, Bounds traveled back to Missouri for a family visit and to hold a meeting in Shelbyville. The meeting lasted for several weeks and was attended by Bishop E. M. Marvin and his wife.

On his way home, Bounds stopped in St. Louis to spend a few days with Bishop Marvin and to visit the St. Paul Methodist Episcopal Church South. Within a few days, Bounds had fallen in love with the people. The challenge of the church was for a leader with a strong hand. Just as Jesus is the Shepherd that leads, so the people of the St. Paul Church needed a leader, not a dictator, to guide them. Marvin offered Bounds a position to pastor this congregation—a church that was beginning to turn its back on God and become a social club—back into sweet fellowship with a loving Father. Before he left St. Louis, Brother Bounds accepted the position, even though it was not a formal assignment at that time.

At the age of forty, E. M. Bounds returned to Eufaula and shared the news that he would be leaving the church there to take a pastorate in St. Louis. The church in Eufaula was strong. They had tripled in size, had a new building that was debt-free, and were sending financial support for missions and ministries throughout the region, regardless of race. In September of 1875 Brother Bounds left Alabama to return home to Missouri.

11

St. Louis

The preacher who is not constantly growing in grace, and growing in the intensity of his desires after God, will rarely advance his people to any spiritual depths or spiritual heights. The one condition of helping other people nearer to God is to have a growing nearness to Him ourselves.

—E. M. Bounds

By mid-September crowds started attending St. Paul's Methodist Church located in the affluent, growing, and prosperous area of St. Louis, as Bounds preached on holy living. The messages were simple yet full of godly wisdom, and they pierced men's souls as they were delivered by a humble man with a generous and compassionate heart for the people.

However, some of the members who had seemed so strong and faithful were leaving to attend other churches because they found the change in leadership to be unsettling. Bounds pointed out that Jesus said, "Every branch in me that beareth not fruit he taketh away: and every branch that beareth fruit, he purgeth it, that it may bring forth more fruit" (John 15:2). Any church that desires to have much healthy fruit must undergo the purging of God's Word that cuts away any part of the church that might contaminate the new fruit. This was contrary to traditional teaching, and emotions ran high when social friends left the fellowship. But the people began to trust their pastor as he led their church with respect and honor for all people. Within the first year the red brick building at 1927 St. Louis Avenue began to be filled to capacity.

With the church experiencing such growth, members began to talk about enlarging the building. However, Brother Bounds wanted to strengthen the fellowship in discipleship training without the distraction of building, so he forestalled any plans for expansion.

Though he was away from Eufaula and absorbed by his new ministry in St. Louis, Bounds could not keep his mind from moving to thoughts of the beautiful Emma Barnett back in Alabama. Letters traveled back and forth between the two until at last Bounds found himself on a train returning to visit this radiant angel that had captured his heart. He eventually sought the father of young Emmie (as she was called), asked for his approval, and a date for the marriage was set.

Bounds returned to St. Louis and his work, while Emmie began to prepare for the wedding. The hot sun of summer gave way to lovely days of fall, and on September 19, 1876, Emma Elizabeth Barnett was married to Edward McKendree Bounds at the First Methodist Church of Eufaula, which Edward had been so instrumental in building. Dr. A. W. Barnett, the bride's father, who was both a minister and a medical doctor, performed the ceremony. A few days later, Bounds, at the age of forty-one, presented his new wife, twenty years his junior, to the congregation of St. Paul's Methodist Church in St. Louis. It was a time of joy and excitement in the church, and the people had nothing but love for their pastor's new wife.

The church continued to grow as the city of St. Louis expanded northward. The community was very family-oriented and on almost any given day the streets would be occupied with baby carriages pushed along by the proud parents of precious children. Emmie Bounds would walk amid the young mothers with excitement and anticipation, for she was now expecting their first child.

Edward and Emmie were excited and thankful to God for this wonderful gift, and they were elated at the prospect of being parents. However, beginning a family was a very private matter for Bounds, and as soon as Emmie began to show signs of her pregnancy, he insisted she remain inside. He did not want her to be seen in public "in her condition."

As the weather began to turn colder, Emmie encouraged her husband to allow her to return to Eufaula for the birth of their child. The milder temperatures would be better for her, and her father would be able to see after her medical needs. So the arrangements were made, and Brother Bounds escorted Emmie back to Alabama to await the blessed event. He then returned to St. Louis until Emmie should call for him to come. Bounds spent the intervening months seeing after the needs of his congregation and praying fervently for his wife and baby. Letters traveled between them often, and at last the telegram came on the last week of October telling Edward to make his way to Eufaula.

The church in St. Louis waited impatiently for news of the impending birth. On November 7, 1877, a telegram arrived announcing the safe arrival of Celeste, a beautiful, healthy daughter. "For this child I prayed; and the Lord hath given me my petition which I asked of him (1 Sam. 1:27).

In the center of the city trouble was brewing in one of the other congregations. The church had turned into itself and had no mission vision. Evangelism was looked upon as an archenemy. Bishop Marvin, in charge of the district, realized there were great problems within the church and decided some changes in assignment would be necessary to turn the church back to God from the social organization it had become. After much prayer and numerous meetings with the pastor, Bishop Marvin was desperate to change the situation. He met with Bounds and asked to move him to the First Methodist Episcopal Church South. In the fall of 1879 Bounds moved his family from the quiet area of Twelfth Street to the heart of the city at the corners of Washington and Eighth Streets.

In the next year Brother Bounds was used mightily of God as he refocused the church to the desire of God's heart. Many years later a memorial to Bounds was presented to the St. Louis Annual Conference in 1912:

> His pastorate in St. Louis not only sifted out the sand and relaid the foundation of the faith of the people, but set a new standard for his brethren in the ministry for holy living and faithful service. There were some triumphs of prayer in those days when he met each week for prayer with Jas. J. Watts and W. R. Mays, fellow pastors. This meant much to him whose discerning spirit once said to this writer, "There are not many preachers with whom you can pray."

In his memoirs of Brother Bounds, Reverend Vaughn shared more of Bounds' time in St. Louis as he wrote,

> He had a genius for the unseen world. Like (Bishop) Marvin, he spoke with the authority of one who lived with God. His was no discussion of scientific theories and philosophers' social problems, but he proclaimed God as imminent in His church to produce holy living. [He preached that] Christ was a present and almighty healer for a diseased soul, and he was God's messenger. In his early ministry, he held his hearers by this gift as well as by his message, but he studiously laid aside all such helps and came, as Paul, "not with excellency of speech

or of wisdom, not with enticing words of man's wisdom, lest the cross of Christ should be made of none effect," and that the word might be in "demonstration of the spirit and of power." But often he was eloquent in spite of himself, as his heart burned under the divine touch of his preaching.

One of Brother Bounds' strongest testimonies among his fellow pastors was that he truly loved the people of his congregation more than preaching or pastoring. He was constantly in the homes of his people, fellowshiping with them and discipling them. He loved his parishioners and preached from the pulpit to meet their needs. The people responded by turning to God or moving to another church, but even those who moved away did so without rebuttal. For they knew their pastor loved them more than his own ministry. He preached that Jesus died on the cross for the souls of men, not for man's calling. He proclaimed men were saved from sin to worship God and to be a blessing to the brethren. He encouraged his members to focus first on God, and then to worship Him in obedience to the Word.

Soon after accepting the challenge of this new church, Emma found she was again "with child." The church was excited for their pastor and his young wife. Bounds was happy that Emma was content to stay the winter in St. Louis during this pregnancy, but insisted again that she remain indoors.

On February 14, 1880, God blessed the Bounds family with another baby daughter, whom they named Corneille. There was much celebration and joy in the church as they welcomed this child into their midst. By springtime families had come from Eufaula, Hannibal, and Shelbyville to see Edward, Emma, Celeste, and Corneille. At age forty-five, Bounds was delighted to be the father of two girls.

After much success at the First Methodist Episcopal

Church South, Bounds was offered the opportunity to return to St. Paul's Methodist Church South. Though unsure of the reason for the move, he quickly accepted and by fall had moved his family and all their household goods to what was now the heart of the city's business center.

Bounds' ministry began to take on a new facet. His presence in the business community had an effect on the merchants and businessmen of that area, for they began to have a new attitude toward their employees. In addition, there was less crime on the streets, as Bounds also prayed for the street people.

On November 30, 1881, Bounds was again in the pulpit of the West Selma (now Church Street) Methodist Church. He had experienced revival in this church during the war and then had pastored it from 1869 to 1871. Now he returned to share the Word of God once again. The house was full each night he spoke. The pastor of the church, Rev. E. L. Loveless, had requested Bounds through the invitation committee because of the lasting effect of his preaching to the congregation in Selma. Even though it had been ten years since Bounds had pastored there, Reverend Loveless could detect his lingering spiritual impact on the people.

For the years following, Brother Bounds continued to pastor and write articles that appeared in the *Advocate* as well as other church and secular newspapers. His writings stirred the hearts and souls of people because they came from a pen without malice or ambition but full of love for God. Each statement made was intended to meet a need of the church or the Christian. Never using an idle word that did not have a spiritual principle, Bounds always used his gifts to bring people to an intimate relationship with God. During this time, the pietistic life-style of Bounds held even his critics in check as they could not speak against a man of such integrity.

As the pastors, bishops, and church leaders became ever sensitive to the writing gift of Brother Bounds, the Joint Committee on Editorial Management approached him and asked him to take a writing and speaking position as Associate Editor of the *St. Louis Christian Advocate* in June 1883.

The first issues of the *Advocate*, after he accepted his new role, found very few of the writings of E. M. Bounds. This was in keeping with his tradition of getting to know people. Bounds spent those first few months visiting the churches in the conference and reporting on the endeavors of the people. This gained him a quick acceptance by the people and the pastors as they got to know this upstanding man of faith.

Soon, however, the cold and snow began to prevent him from traveling. Bounds was not unhappy, nevertheless, for his precious Emma was expecting their third child. As winter began to pass, the word was spread that God had entrusted to the Bounds family a son. On the twenty-fourth day of February, 1884, Edward Bounds was welcomed into the world. Little Edward was a very special treat to his big sisters as well as to his parents. The girls were told, however, that they had to be very gentle with their new brother, for he was a weak and sickly child.

Throughout the year, Bounds continued to be very busy building a foundation of fellowship with his constituents. In April he was able to participate in the thirteenth session of the Chillicothe District Conference. Rev. John Anderson, the presiding elder and a dear friend, had asked Bounds to come and share in the conference. This allowed him to preach each night in his old church. It was while pastoring in Brunswick that Bounds had been arrested during the war. A significant movement occurred as preachers like Rev. M. B. Chapman, Rev. P. E. Plattsburg, Dr. Hendrix, and E. M. Bounds preached in churches throughout the community each night.

Bounds also found himself in the very joyful situation of reporting on a great meeting to be held by his dear evangelist friend Sam Jones, who was coming to St. Louis to hold a crusade. The Sunday morning service would be held at the Centenary Methodist Church. In the evening the meeting would be held in the largest auditorium in the St. Louis region, Merchants Esporitin Music Hall.

Bounds and Jones spent many days reminiscing about the great meetings in Alabama and Georgia. Both men were very much in the mindset of John and Charles Wesley, so that they found common foundation for strong and deep fellowship, which would later prove to be of great importance to both men. It was from this bonding that the two would be highly involved in the *Tennessee Advocate*, which would later influence their lives.

At this time the Bounds family was faced with a decision about a trip scheduled over Christmas. A dear friend who had recently moved to Atlanta wanted Bounds to perform his marriage to a childhood sweetheart who was a good friend of Emmie's. The wedding was to take place in New York in the home of the bride's parents. Emmie wanted so badly to go to New York and see her friend married, and Uncle Charley and Aunt Margaret had already agreed to keep the children in Kirksville, where the children loved to visit. But Emmie's health was poor.

Finally the decision was made to take the whole family to Eufaula, where Emmie's father could give her some sound medical attention. The Bounds family moved into the second floor of the home on Broad Street where Emmie had grown up. Bounds stayed a short time and then boarded a train for New York—alone. Emmie was unable to travel. Bounds particularly hated to leave her, knowing how much she wanted to go to New York, see the city, and be with her friend on such an important occasion. Upon reaching New York, Bounds performed the wedding, and then caught the first train south to rejoin his family.

When he arrived in Eufaula, he received news that Emmie had taken a turn for the worse. He found his dear wife very sick and weak. He stayed at her bedside, reading to her from the Word of God, praying, making plans for the future, as they enjoyed each other's company. Soon, however, her condition became critical. Though Bounds tried to shield the children, they sensed their mother was very ill. Throughout the church families, prayers went up for dear Emmie—prayers for her healing, but also for God's will for this lovely young mother, wife, and saint of God. In February Emmie began to bask in the light from the throne room of God.

Funeral services for Emma Elizabeth Bounds would be held in the church building she had been married in and her husband had helped to construct. Her casket was carried north to the main street of town and the Fairview Cemetery. The headstone was lovingly inscribed:

EMMIE BARNETT
wife of
Rev. E. M. Bounds
Entered Heaven
February 18, 1886
Age 30
A PURE, SIMPLE, LOVELY LIFE
CROWNED WITH A TRIUMPHANT DEATH

The trip back to St. Louis was hard for the Bounds family. Leaving the body of Emmie behind, Bounds gathered his children close to him and prayed for guidance for their future. When he arrived home, co-workers from the *Advocate* were there to help. Also, Bounds' brother

Charles and oldest sister, Harriet, had come from Keyetesville to take care of the children and suggested they
go home with them. This was a workable arrangement,
for the children loved their Uncle Charles and Aunt Harriet. Harriet's middle name was Sophronia, and the children affectionately called her Aunt Phronie.

These days were a time of growing for Bounds. Without Emmie, and separated from his children, he threw
himself into his work with a vengeance. His first article
that appeared in the *Advocate* after Emmie's death was
a tribute, printed on March 3, 1886:

IN MEMORY

Emmie Barnett Bounds, daughter of Dr. A. W. Barnett,
wife of E. M. Bounds, died in Eufaula, Alabama, February 18, 1886, in the thirtieth year of her life. "Mine has
been a short life, but a very happy one," she said to her
father, "short when measured by years, long when measured by goodness."

Emmie had a most pleasing and persuasive manner,
a faculty which entered natively and with ease into
every circle, a vivacity which never declined: her love
was always virgin, her spirits always fresh and rosy. She
combined the artless purity of a child with the dignity
and grace of a woman. A quick, acute, and playsome
fancy, a strong tenacious will with no mixture of obsti-
nacy or self.

For nine years, she brightened my life and the shadows came at her going: shadows which are relieved but
not lifted by the rich legacy of deathless, tearful, holy
memories which she left.

Her tastes were simple and unworldly: her faith clear
and strong, without doubt or dimness. Her experience,
molded after that of the early Methodists and early
Christians, was confiding, assuring, rapturous, fre-
quently convulsing her whole frame with ecstatic emo-
tion as if filled with new wine. She did not seek these

seasons, they came like the blush and bloom of spring, spontaneously, inevitably, as the product of a true, hearty, and joyous faith; often finding expression in the favorite stanza of a favorite hymn:

> O would He more of heaven bestow!
> And let the vessel break;
> And let my ransomed spirit go,
> To grasp the God I seek;
> In rapturous awe on Him to gaze,
> Who bought the sight for me,
> And shout, and wonder at His grace,
> To all eternity.

She had the most self-denying jealousy of my work and under the most trying conditions would make no claim on my time or service, holding me and my work sacred for the Lord. When I informed her of the kindness of Dr. M'Anally and Mr. Dameron in strongly and tenderly urging me to lay aside all considerations and care for business and devote myself to her, she said, "I am very thankful and greatly comforted by that, I need to be in no hurry to die, now."

For more than four weeks her dearest friends were not permitted to see her, and there were many long and painful seasons in which no one but myself could be in her room, as she was too weak and nervous to bear the slightest pressure. The religious services had to be of the simplest and most informal kind; a scripture, a question, a verse from our standard hymnal, a sentence of prayer, as her condition demanded or allowed.

Her sister, fearing this simple service might upset her, made the inquiry. Emmie replied, "No, they refresh me and come into my life with a new and higher force. I look to them more than to medicine to relieve my pain." And she said to me, "I am too weak to repent or follow well what you say, but a sweet voice seems to repeat them to me all night long and they flow through my soul." Death found her ready, willing, longing to go. "My work is done," she said, "I would not undertake it again. I have done nothing; I rely on the merits of Jesus Christ as my Saviour."

The things of God and heaven had always been the real things to her. Ever relishing with keen delight the pure and sweet things of earth, but they were only the flowers and sunshine that brightened the way which led to the permanent and real. Her reference to heaven during her sickness was not occasional but continual—the theme of the most familiar, constant, and happy converse between us. Her longings to be with Christ were not fitful or feeble but strong, ardent, full, and deep in their flowing; destroying all fear, retiring the strongest and dearest earthly love, and expressed without intermission or hesitancy, bearing her constantly in the exalted regions of a triumphant faith.

To her eagerness to go, sometimes bordering on impatience, I would interpose a check. She would for a moment be most resigned with a peaceful attitude. "Every day is Sabbath to me," she said. Referring to her anxiety to go, she said, "It does not arise from my suffering nor in submission," and took up the stanza of a favorite hymn and I finished it for her,

Tis not that murmuring thoughts arise
And dreads a Father's will:
Tis not that meek submission flies,
And would not suffer still.
It is that heaven-born faith surveys
The path that leads to light,
And longs her eagle plumes to raise
And lose itself in sight.
It is that hope with ardor glows
To see Him face to face,
Whose dying love language knows
Sufficient art to trace.

To this she smiled and nodded approval: it made up the sum and reason of her seeming impatience. The last quotation I heard from her was a labored effort to articulate the last stanza of *Rock of Ages*. The last intelligible phrase she uttered, as I bent low to catch her whisper, was "the texts," and while I repeated her two favorite ones, John 11:25–26 and 1 Corinthians 15:52–57, her soul preened its wings and took heavenly flight.

I learned from her, not by experience, how I might have been hindered in my work by a wife who was not in fullest and most unselfish harmony within. She taught me by experience how a devoted wife, maintaining supreme loyalty to Jesus Christ, could in many ways and at all points be very helpful. I learned from her how in the elevated forms of faith, the strongest and purest type of wifely and motherly love is almost dissolved in the presence of the more engaging and authoritative attractions of the heavenly world.

May the voice which called and clothed her for the sublimer service of heaven, fit and perfect me for the earthly service.

Angels, let the ransomed stranger
In your tender care be blessed,
Hoping, trusting, safe from danger
Till the trumpet end her rest.
Till the trump, which shakes creation,
Through the ceiling heavens shall roll,
Till the day of consummation,
Till the bridal of the soul.

12

His Walk in the Valley

No one knows what you and I
Are keeping in the heart,
The hopes and fears that hidden lie—
Of life a potent part.
The world may look upon the face
Nor guess their hidden woes,
Nor can it there our pleasures trace—
We've much that no one knows.
No one knows the unbreathed prayer
We're hiding in the breast,
None see the hope stars shining there,
Nor clouds of dark unrest.
None view the unseen battlefield
Where wrongs the right oppose,
Our inner lives are not revealed—
We've much that no one knows.

—Selected

As Edward McKendree Bounds walked through the valley of the shadow of death with his dear Emmie, he found himself no stranger to valleys. He had walked through the valley of trial and temptation in the gold mines of California, the courthouses of Missouri, and the bloodstained ground of the South. And now through the life and death of Emmie he had learned more about trust, faith, obedience, dependence, and love.

Though the view from the peak of a glorious mountain may offer a tremendous look into distant lands, the majestic trees will not grow there. The mountaintop is a place sought by those who seek solitude and meditation. Many philosophers, and even some Christians, seek the mountaintops for a closer communion with God. But just as the strongest trees are found in the valleys rather than the mountaintops, so God uses the valleys to strengthen His children. Just as the trees are strengthened by resistance to storms, wind, rain, and intense heat, so the child of God is strengthened by resistance to pain, suffering, and tribulation.

The trees that grow in shallow soil grow rapidly and beautifully, but they have weak roots and they are easily blown away. Christians can be fed all the proper nutrients. Many receive training, attend Bible studies, prayer meetings, and learn to look and sound like a true believer, but their faith is put to the test when the winds of doubt blow, and many have no roots in the Lord Jesus Christ. The trials of life did not shake the faith of E. M. Bounds, but instead drove him closer to the Savior. He had been tested, and only God knew the task that lay ahead for this prophet of prayer.

When Emmie lay on her bed of affliction, many friends, neighbors, and supporters came to visit. One was Dr. Luther M. Smith, President of Southern University in Greensboro, Alabama. Dr. Smith had first heard of Bounds in the testimony of Dr. William M. Wightman, the former president of Southern University. Dr. Wightman told of a chaplain who had come into town with a group of Confederate soldiers from Missouri in the midst of the war. He said the chaplain was thin in body but strong in the Word of God; poor in goods yet held the riches of eternity by his faith in God. The testimony of God's grace and how it was poured out on the community through this young chaplain was still spoken of in the churches and halls of the university. Dr. Luther Smith requested this special man, E. M. Bounds, be given an Honorary Doctorate of Divinity degree from the university.

It was with great gratitude and deep conviction that Bounds turned down this special honor. He felt a Christian should avail himself of education and that lack of study was no excuse for ignorance of God's Word. Indeed, he tried to send all of his children to college and emphasized an education program in every church he pastored. However, he felt a degree from a university was a recognition from man and had the potential of becoming a sought after recognition. He was concerned that degrees might take the place of seeking God's righteousness, and church leaders might begin to be sought based on their educational title rather than on God's guidance and approval.

Dr. Smith humbly accepted Bounds' response and asked him instead to come for a week of meetings around graduation time. Bounds quickly agreed. The meeting was to be held in April, a good time for Bounds, for though his heart still grieved for Emmie, his children were settled. It was as though the community was ready to explode, such was its expectation of the Holy Spirit's movement. However, the meeting started rather slowly. It seemed the people expected the movement of God to come from Bounds rather than from God himself. Bounds continued to pray.

Soon a holy awareness began to fall on the community, and the people became afraid of coming to the meeting with unconfessed sin in their life. The drawing of the Holy Spirit was so strong that businesses began to close early to allow everyone to attend. It was as if the gates that held back the Holy Spirit had been burst by the tears of repentant souls. On May 2, 1886, the *Alabama Christian Advocate* ran this announcement:

Greensboro—Some revival indications have been reported. A revival of marvelous power has visited Greensboro Station. Brother Dickinson and his yokefellows here have much to prompt the joyous exclamation "God hath done great things for us!" The Spirit's presence in quickening, convicting power was not limited to the walls of the Southern University, but went forth in remarkable demonstrations through the entire community. Old and young felt most positively that God was indeed in the midst of Israel.

From day to day, and from night to night, congregations eagerly thronged the sanctuary of the Most High. Penitents of all ages crowded the altar, earnestly inquiring the way of life, and occasionally even the midnight hour found them struggling for pardon. Conversions were clear, joyous, and after the New Testament type. Sixty-two were received into church last Sunday morning. One hundred conversions have been reported, and there will be others.

The meetings lasted through the summer and slacked up until the crops had been harvested, then again the surge of the Holy Spirit drew people to the altars. During the first weeks of the meeting, Bounds was again approached about receiving a Doctor of Divinity degree. Then, without his knowledge, he was given the degree during the 1886 graduation ceremonies. This was a great embarrassment to Brother Bounds, but he did not wish to hinder the movement of God nor place the university president in an awkward position. At a later time it was shared with Bounds that it was given because of his humility and because of the work God had done through him. "By humility and fear of the Lord are riches, and honor, and life" (Prov. 22:4). Years later Dr. J. R. Vaughn wrote the following account surrounding Bounds' degree from the Southern University:

He was without ambition for honors. In any form

they were distasteful. When, unknown and undesired by him, the degree of D.D. was conferred upon him, he was embarrassed that he must carry the title all his days. Shortly after this event, as we sat together at the table of Rev. Felix R. Hill, our hostess addressed Bounds as "Doctor." He looked up with a pained expression and said, "Sister Hill, if you love me, call me Brother Bounds." He felt that these titles were borrowed from the customs of the world and had no place among the followers of Jesus, who "sought not honors of one another."

Bounds personal life also made a blessed advance. Though pain and weakness often blurred Emmie's mind as she lay on her deathbed, her love for her husband and children was ever foremost in her thoughts. She shared with her family at that time her desire that her husband marry her cousin Hattie Barnett from Washington, Georgia. She was concerned about who would raise her children and care for the man of her heart. The person she most trusted and desired to carry on in her place was her closest friend and cousin, Hattie.

As time passed, Bounds made the trip to Washington, Georgia, according to Emmie's wishes, to meet her cousin Harriet. He was fascinated by this small town, where men such as Jesse Mercer, John A. Broadus, Daniel Marshall, Sam Jones, Shubal Stearns, and Luther Rice were held in high esteem and had great influence. Among these fine men was Samuel Barnett, the brother of A. W. Barnett and the father of Harriet. Samuel Barnett was the first railroad commissioner in the state of Georgia, and a very powerful but humble man.

Emmie's insight proving absolutely correct, Brother Bounds continued his relationship with Harriet into the spring of 1887. The summer found them making plans for marriage, and on September 5, 1887, E. M. Bounds sat at his desk in St. Louis and penned the following letter to Dr. A. W. Barnett:

Dear Doctor,

Saturday week I took the children to my brother Charley's at Kirksville. They enjoyed the trip. It took a day—nearly 204 miles. Edward holds you very strongly. He cannot get it out of his mind to go to Grandpa's. He talks of Ben. I preached in Kirksville, day and night. He stayed with my brother very well during morning service, but he settled at night that he was going with me in to the pulpit, and before we reached the church, some distance, he separated from Charley and would not let him take his hand but clung to me. I did not understand it till we separated. As I went up into the pulpit, Edward raised the congregation by declaring his purpose in a loud voice to go with me. He did it twice. My brother then quieted him.

He kept untying his cloak scarf on the trains. I said, "Edward, you should not do that."

He replied, "Papa, this belongs to me. It does not belong to you."

The children are well, busy, and sweet. I will go up to see them tonight and return tomorrow night to the Missouri Conference.

The girls and Aunt Jule thought it best for Hattie and I to take the children at once rather than wait till spring. We will follow their desires, though we expected to let them stay with their friends. But it is better as they suggested. I am sorry that they will be so far from you.

Hattie and I are very anxious for you to marry us. I do hope you will consider it. The trip would help you and we would be delighted. I do hope, though, if it will be impossible, that you will contact me. About the 18th or 20th of October will be the time. I do and ever shall hold you in the highest regard and tenderest love. My prayers are always for you—my life has been sweetly blessed in your house. I have been made very happy and better by my darling Emmie. Love to Cousin Dell, and kiss the baby Reese and Annie.

In Love,
E. M. Bounds

On October, 25, 1887, Dr. A. W. Barnett married E. M. Bounds to Harriet A. Barnett in the little red brick Methodist church on Liberty Street in Washington, Georgia. The church was filled to overflowing as many gathered to wish this couple the best for their future.

This was quite a step, both for Bounds and for Harriet, who was called Hattie. She was faced with an instant family, made easier only by the fact that all the children loved her already. She had great respect for her new husband and always referred to him as "Doctor," and taught her children to do so as well. Apparently by now Edward was accustomed to the title.

Edward realized the heavy burden placed on this thirty-year-old southern belle. He was also confronted with the fact that at fifty-two years of age, he could possibly begin a new family.

After the wedding, the couple traveled with the children for a time of vacation, and then visited with friends and family in Eufaula before returning to St. Louis. When they arrived home, Aunt Phronie (Bounds' sister, Harriet Sophronia Bounds Vandeventer) and Aunt Fannie (Bounds' sister Francis Amelia Bounds Lowens) had moved to St. Louis from Keyetesville to help the children make the adjustment to their new life. These aunts had taken care of the children since Emmie's death. The Bounds family moved into a new three-story house, ample to accommodate everyone.

The year 1888 began with great excitement as the announcement was made that God would bless the family with a new baby. On July 4, Samuel Barnett Bounds arrived, quite an Independence Day celebration!

The year also brought challenges to Bounds in his work. His writing was appearing in more and more newspapers. His editorials were clear as he continued to stand for God's righteousness in the church. Piety and discipline became his hallmark. In his opinion, the current call by many in the church for change was nothing more than a disguise allowing a compromise with the world. While the church embraced the world, seeking to draw people to church, Bounds stood firm in preaching that when Jesus Christ is high and lifted up, He will draw people unto himself.

The clouds of a storm had formed by the time of the Methodist Episopal National Conference in 1890. Many wanted the *Christian Advocate* in Nashville to take a stand on worldliness. The debate on management and editorial style was heated but remained Christian in attitude. However, when the voting began, the position of assistant editor was vacated when the nomination to retain J. W. Boswell did not carry. Nominations were made several times without any man receiving a majority. Finally, on the fourth vote, Dr. E. M. Bounds was elected to the assistant editor position. The next vote was for the editor's position, held by a veteran of the paper, Dr. O. P. Fitzgerald, who many felt should retire. When the vote to retain was counted, Dr. Fitzgerald resigned to retire. The vote to fill that position was filled on the first ballot by Dr. Hoss.

As soon as Dr. Bounds returned to St. Louis, he began to prepare to move to Nashville, where he would begin his new job on June 7, 1890. In the *St. Louis Advocate*, Bounds entered this statement:

In the July 4, 1883 issue of the *Advocate* this announcement appeared: "With this number begins my relations, my duties, my responsibilities, as associate editor of the *Advocate*. E. M. Bounds"

With this issue these relations, duties, and responsibilities end. The church has ordered me elsewhere; the soldier has nothing to do with sentiment, choice, or preferences; his vocation is to fight, his law to obey. I am debtor to the readers of the *Advocate* for their patience, criticism, and appreciated prayers.

At this point of review and change, I raise my Ebenezer; for the future, the Lord will provide.

As soon as the formal notice came to Bounds in St. Louis, he prepared his family and sent them to Washington, Georgia. Hattie was soon to deliver their second child. Though he loved his new mother, young Edward was having trouble adjusting to the loss of his own mother. In Washington, Hattie had a private room while she was pregnant. She was not even allowed to see the children, but she would often sneak little Edward into her room and he would sleep close to her bed. There he would be emotionally comforted, even as his physical health continued to deteriorate.

On July 11, 1890, another boy was added to the Bounds family. He was named after his Uncle Charles in Missouri. Bounds, at the age of fifty-five, found himself in the middle of a changing ministry and a rapidly growing family.

The joy of the new birth was overshadowed by the now critical health problems of young Edward Bounds. Less than two weeks after the birth of Charles, little Edward died. The family was grief-stricken. "He will swallow up death in victory; and the Lord God will wipe away tears from off all faces" (Isa. 25:8).

The question as to where to bury little Edward arose when Bounds desired his son should be carried to Eufaula and buried with his mother. He wired Dr. A. W. Barnett and asked about the need to bury young Edward there. Dr. Barnett wrote back that the child should remain in Washington and be buried in the Barnett family plot. For Edward to be buried in Washington was what Hattie wanted, for she had come to love the child as her own in the three years since her marriage to Dr. Bounds. So on July 26 the little casket was lowered into the ground at the entrance of the Barnett family plot. On the base of the stone marker are the words: PERFECT FOREVER.

Bounds penned the following letter to Dr. Barnett shortly afterward:

My Dear Doctor Barnett,

Your kindly sympathetic letter was duly received and fulfilled its gracious mission.

I came at once to bury our dear little Edward. My first inclination as to his sickness was the telegram announcing his death on Wednesday. I arrived here Thursday. The rain was so hard and so incessant that we could only deposit his body in a vault, expecting to bury him Friday or Saturday. The weather has been so raging that we will postpone his burial until tomorrow. The point of carrying him to Eufaula was in my mind and raised by the family here. His natural burial place would be beside his dear mother, and had he died up the country I would have taken him there, but he was here. Hattie was anxious for him to sleep here. Your family is leaving Eufaula. The visits of the children, Hattie, and myself will in the very nature of things be oftener to Washington than to Eufaula, and the fact of a long trip and the attachment of the family here, and that they had already arranged his burial here, decided me to let the dear body of our precious boy sleep here.

His devotion to Hattie was the most beautiful thing I ever knew. It had in it the tenderness of a lover, the grace of a manly love, the fondest obedience of a son. He begged to be carried to her while sick and he did spend one day in her room.

He was almost a perfect boy and he had often talked to me of doing my work when I was gone to heaven. He said to Hattie, "When I think of my mother in heaven, I have to shut my eyes." The blow is heavy on me, my heart seems literally broken. I rejoice in the will of God, its wisdom and love, but my heart is broken by the blow. It seems to spread full force over me. He was so dear to me and so full of life, the perfection of a boy. I am sure it is a call to me for intense effort and deeper consecration. I will heed by God's grace, and on me it may be an effectual call to Christ. I will return to Nashville Wednesday or Thursday. . . .

I may not have the heart or strength to write to Celeste and Corneille before I go. Hattie will write to them as soon as she is able. I send thankful, caring kisses and much love to Cousin Dell, Anna, Reese, Eunice, Uncle Willis, and Aunt Jule.

God is calling our hearts to Him as He takes our treasures. With much love and continuous prayers,

E. M. Bounds

Grief and the need for help with the children kept Hattie in Washington, Georgia. Bounds and Dr. Barnett would make frequent visits home, as young Charles was also a sickly child. Just one year and eight days after his birth, baby Charles returned to his heavenly Father. Charles would be buried close to his brother.

As soon as the family settled down, Bounds finally moved them to Nashville. There they enjoyed the beauty of the city as fall brought new colors to the trees and a crispness in the air that was refreshing and needful to this bereaved family. There God's healing and comforting hand applied the Balm of Gilead to their hearts.

13

Life in Nashville

Why should I fear tomorrow?
The Lord directs my way.
Why should I trouble borrow?
I live but for today.
Whenever I am weary,
In God I find my rest,
And when my path seems dreary,
I know its for the best.

—E. M. Bounds
(First published in the
New York Observer)

As his family life became calmer, Bounds' work became more difficult. Controversy was brewing regarding the calling of vocational evangelists. Many felt they should not preach in church meetings, but in camp meetings only. They believed the evangelists were not interested in the stability of the church flock and upset the pastors' work. This was extremely disturbing to Brother Bounds. He believed God worked in special ways through men with the gift of evangelism. His support of the evangelist was often attributed not to his convictions but to his personal fellowship with Rev. Sam Jones, an evangelist with an orphanage in Decatur, Georgia. A struggle had developed regarding church assignments going to those men, with certain convictions and labels being placed on men, including Bounds, regarding their Wesleyan convictions on living a holy, Spirit-filled life of service.

While traveling from one conference to another, Bounds saw the frustrations of ministers who had more training, materials, and facilities than ever before but without the power they so desperately sought. This led to one of Bounds' first articles on the subject. Following is an excerpt:

THE PREACHER—HIS POWER

The power of preaching lies in the fact that it sows the life-giving, imperishable seed of God's Word. Only the Word of God has this life-giving energy; beautiful thoughts, fine sentiments, striking and true statements of philosophy, poetry, or genius have no life of God in them. The preacher may gain reputation, popularity, influence by these, but the power to quicken and convict consciences, to perfect holiness, and colonize heaven; to do effectively what God designs the preacher to do, will depend on his trueness to God's Word. The more simply and earnestly the preacher becomes the mouthpiece of God, the more diligently he feeds on the Word of God by meditation and prayer, and gives it out as the mother gives out her life to her babe, the more will his legitimate power be enhanced. Modern preachers too often know too many books better than they know the Bible; are more alive to the words of man than to the words of God. These men have the power of man's words, which is sometimes a strange, marvelous, and beautiful power, but powerless against sin, powerless to radiate and perfect holiness. . . .

The power of preaching lies in the strength of the preacher's faith. Faith is the mightiest and among the rarest of principles. Much of that which goes currently as faith, by a close spiritual analysis would be found to contain but a small ingredient of that precious article. Faith does the mightiest things, it has no limit but omnipotence. The roll of its results recorded in Hebrews is without parallel, and these results are to be more than duplicated in the realms of spiritual work by the stronger faith of the gospel. The preacher must believe with a mighty faith, a faith that is never disturbed by fear, never darkened by doubt; a faith that never sees the seen, but which fills its eye and heart with the unseen and eternal; a faith which sees nothing but God, seeks nothing but God, believes nothing but God; a faith which makes the unseen things the real things, and counts the seen as low, distrustful, perishing. . . .

The power of the preacher lies in his power of prayer, in his ability to pray so as to reach God, and bring great results. The power of prayer is rarely tested, its possibilities seldom understood, never exhausted. The pulpit fixed and fired with holy desires on God, with a tireless faith, will be the pulpit of power. Nothing is so feeble, so insipid, so resultless as a little vapid praying. To pray over our sermons like we say grace over our meals does no good. Every step of the sermon should be born of the throes of prayer, its beginning and end should be vocal with the plea and song of prayer. Its delivery should be impassioned and driven by the power of prayer.

Prayer with fire of intense desire, urged by faith that folds not its wings till God is reached, is the mightiest of forces. Prayer that carries heaven by storm, that moves God by a relentless advocacy, these make the pulpit a throne, its deliverances like the decrees of destiny. The power of preaching must always be backed by a Christly life; the preacher's every act a sermon; his life the Bible illustrated, his holiness without mixture, white and aflame. In the manner, measure, or grade of his utterances, no semblance of the world must be found, no points of worldly contact or stain. The life he lives, the life of heaven on earth. He comes to this position by a great cost, by a costly death; but he comes to it, or he comes not to his power.

When the Alabama Conference began in January 1892, Bounds was offered the position of editor of the *Alabama Christian Advocate*. The Alabama Conference was also in controversy. The Alabama Publishing Committee was a new committee when it met with the *Advocate* committee. Bounds was voted on unanimously, but he refused the office. Reverend Thomas Armstrong was elected to the post. Many of Bounds' critics accused him of being ambitious and seeking the office of editor. However, the entire action had been completely unsolicited by Bounds and he would not even respond to such accusations.

In response to many questions and concerns raised at the Alabama Conference, Brother Bounds penned the following article:

HINDERS PREACHING

Among the things that hinder spiritual results, fine preaching must have a place among the first. Fine preaching is that kind of preaching where the force of the preacher is expended to make the sermon great in thought, tasteful as a work of art, perfect as a scholarly production, complete in rhetorical finish, fine in its pleasing and popular force. In true preaching, the sermon proceeds out of the man; it is part of him, the outflowing of his life. Fine preaching separates between the man and the sermon; he may be the architect, he may build it, but the preacher and the sermon are two. More than this, it separates between the Holy Ghost and the sermon. Such sermons will make an impression, but it is not the impression that the Holy Ghost makes. Influence it may have, but the influence is not distinctly spiritual, if spiritual at all. They do not reach the conscience, are not aimed at it. Some other part of the nature aside from the more easily reached, bearing more pleasant fruit than an awakened conscience, draws the arrow from this polished quiver. The preacher has made too much of the sermon, the sermon has made too much of the preacher; the hearer has made too much of the preacher *and* the sermon for either the Holy Ghost or the conscience to make much of either. . . .

The wisdom of words, even their persuasive beauty, abate the power of the gospel. The ends of the gospel cannot be secured by oratory, by rhetoric, by logic, by any kind of tasteful, scholarly statement. More than that, these distract from the essential effects of the gospel, and if the true ends of the gospel are not wholly lost by this "excellent speech" or "enticing words," the results are enfeebled and reduced to a losing minimum. Christ did not choose orators, philosophers, rabbis, scribes to preach His gospel, but unlearned, common men, of common education with common talent and common sense. The gospel is not to be propelled by the intellect, but by the heart. The Holy Ghost resides not in the intellect but in the heart.

A statement of this kind is not to be used in the defense of either ignorance or laziness. No man ought to be wiser than God's preacher. Wise in the wisdom that God gives, wise in the wisdom of following God's plan, submitting to and obeying God's will; none more learned than he, learned in the things of God the preacher must be. Learned in the things of his own heart, none a greater student than he, none more industrious than he absorbed in God's work, and in caring for God's sheep he must "give himself wholly to prayer and the ministry of the Word." Absorbed he will be in studying God's Word, intent on securing that personal nearness and likeness to Christ which will insure the full measure of success; giving his life for God's sheep; happy in suffering or doing God's will, incessant in proclaiming God's Word. The preacher will find his time and strength engrossed, and will have neither time nor taste for the vanities or glare of secular eloquence; these will be a part and portion of that world which he has forsworn. His sermons will flow out of him as the issuance of those streams which have flowed into and filled him from the throne of God. His sermons of him a part. A living life not manufactured by square and rule and compass but born into being, the incorruptible Word of God that liveth and abideth forever.

This article found its way into the hearts of many of those who subscribed to the *Advocate*. A great cry emerged from many who wished to return to Spirit-filled preaching. With the resounding response to this article, God led Brother Bounds to pen yet another article that addressed and struck at the heart of the proper focus and emphasis in ministry. The following article ran on February 18, 1892:

A PRAYERFUL MINISTRY

God's true preachers have been distinguished by one feature—they were men of prayer. Differing often in many things, they have always had a common center. They may have started from different points, and traveled by different roads, but they converged to one point. They were one in prayer. God to them was the center of attraction; and prayer the path that led to God. These men prayed not occasionally, not a little at regular or at odd times, but they so prayed that it entered into and shaped their characters. They so prayed as to affect their own lives and the lives of others; they so prayed as to make the history of the Church and influence the current of the times. They spent much time in prayer, not because they marked the shadow on the dial or the hands on the clock, but because it was to them so momentous and engaging a business that they could scarcely give over. . . .

The praying which makes a prayerful ministry is not a little praying put in, as we put flavor in to give something a pleasant smack, but praying must be in the body, and form the blood and bones. Prayer is no petty duty put into a corner, no piecemeal performance made out of

anything we do should be the result of prayer

the fragments of time which have been snatched from business and other engagements of life, but it means the best of time; the heart of our time and strength must be given. It does not mean the closet absorbed in the study, or swallowed up in the activities of ministerial duties, but it means the closet first, the study and activities second, both study and activities freshened and made efficient by the closet. Prayer that affects one's ministry must give tone to one's life. The praying which gives color and bent to character is no pleasant, hurried pastime. It must enter as strongly into the heart and life as Christ's "strong crying and tears" did; must draw out the soul into an agony of desire as Paul's did; must be an inwrought fire and force like the effectual fervent prayer of James; must be of that quality which when put into the golden censor and incensed before God, works mighty spiritual throes and revolutions. . . .

The superficial results of many a ministry, the deadness of others, is to be found in the lack of praying. The text, the sermon should be the result of prayer. The study should be bathed in prayer; all its duties impregnated with prayer; its whole spirit, the spirit of prayer. "I am sorry that I have prayed so little" was the deathbed regret of one of God's chosen ones. A sad and remorseful regret for a preacher. "I want a life of greater, deeper, truer prayer," said the late Archbishop Tait. So may we all say, and this may we all secure.

While Bounds was in Birmingham, dealing with the committee of the *Advocate*, his family was staying with Dr. Barnett in Eufaula. It was during this time that Hattie became unable to travel because she was with child. On February 29, 1892, the Bounds family was blessed with the birth of a son, Osborne.

As soon as they were able to travel, the family returned to Nashville, where they would settle down for a while. Bounds' activities continued to escalate. Requests for him to speak came pouring in. His writing also was in great demand as he focused on a movement that was sweeping the nation and called for holiness in living. This strict and pietistic preacher was often invited to speak in camp meetings.

Bounds was a featured writer of the *Tennessee Methodist Paper*, the state paper of Tennessee, which also featured Sam Jones, who shared his insights on a deeper walk with God. The editor of that paper was Rev. B. F. Haynes, who had been converted in the Franklin church, where Brother Bounds had pastored after the war.

At the age of fifty-eight, Bounds once again became a father. On September 12, 1893, Hattie presented Bounds with a beautiful daughter. Elizabeth Bounds was born in Washington, Georgia, and her birth was cause of great celebration for the entire family.

The next spring the Twelfth General Conference was held in Memphis, Tennessee. There were many storms brewing within the denomination, and Bounds left Nashville on May 6 to be at the Conference when it opened. The day was bright, but storm clouds lay on the horizon as he arrived. When he checked into the Peabody Hotel, he was greeted by many friends, and they had a wonderful time of fellowship. Many of the bishops and preachers had come to the conference early and led in Wednesday night prayer services in the local churches. An air of testimony was prevalent.

Bishop Hargrove called the 2,500 participants to prayer and to order, and then the business began. The church was packed to capacity. The North Georgia delegation could not even be seated for the press, both Christian and secular, who had gathered in expectation of controversy. They were quite disappointed at first, as the fellowship and good preaching kept the participants with high hopes that God would intervene and intercede in the difficulties.

As rain moved in on the third day of the conference,

spirits remained high. What the rain could not quench, however, the information in the reports could. There were many different emphases, but some that particularly troubled Bounds because he had worked so diligently both preaching and writing to expose the worldly ways that he felt were compromising the denomination.

The committee on revival made a report that would radically change the office of vocational evangelist. They would be under control of their regional conference and could not travel outside the region without written approval. This was a minority report with only eleven signatures affixed. Instead of seeking the will of God concerning the use of a particular evangelist, a church or pastor would have to seek written approval. Many were upset that a small group of people were able to control the church on this issue. Some speculated that this report was a response to evangelists like D. L. Moody and Sam Jones, who others felt were stripping the churches financially and had salaries that were much too large.

Another raging controversy broke out as one of the bishops addressed the "Holiness and Methodist" question. He suggested the solution might be to exclude from the fellowship any person who was involved in the movement. He also proposed the church control all papers using the Methodist title. Bounds felt this was an encroachment on the liberty of the believer, that openness was needed to correctly judge the ways the church was to follow. He also believed a paper not of God would die.

Often during the conference, doors would be closed for private meetings, which also upset Bounds. He felt God's business was always open for scrutiny, and no person should be discussed without that person being present. He believed that confronting people in love would bring credibility to the accusations, healing to the offenses, and repentance to offenders. Even during the Civil War, appointments made in private often stemmed from personal ambition or to elevate friends and not for the good of the whole. He feared this trend within the church, feeling it was dangerous, and the issue burned at his heart.

Yet another conflict emerged on the conference floor when the Tucker Act was brought up. This was a seedbed of discord within the Methodist Church. It began when President Lincoln had signed an order on April 24, 1863, exempting churches, hospitals, and schools from the hostilities of war. The Southern Methodist Publishing House in Nashville, however, had been used extensively by the Union forces and many in the church felt the government should pay remuneration. Dr. Barbee was a strong proponent for the measure, which began shortly after the war. Bounds and Dr. Hoss, editor of the *National Advocate*, both stood against such claims. Bounds felt any payment from the government would have strings attached to it, and the church should not be in subjection or obligation to the government. (His fears were justifiable, for when lobbyists were later hired to obtain these funds, the claim was determined to be excessive. This was quite embarrassing for the church, and was discussed for years.)

Dr. Barbee had led the publishing house to make great profit by printing the Southern Baptist Sunday school materials. People praised Barbee's ability to merchandise. But Bounds felt the profit should be used to purchase Bibles for missions to the Indians, not to strengthen a banking account or a profit statement.

There were other matters that weighed heavily on the heart of this dear prophet of God during this conference. One was the move for unity between the various Methodist factions. Bounds felt there would have to be compromises to reach unity and he knew God's Word must never be compromised. The other was a move to remove Vanderbilt University from church ownership. Bounds felt this was not in keeping with the desires of the people who had sacrificed so much to build the school.

After the conference, Bounds caught the first train back to Nashville. In his suit pocket was a paper he had spent the night in agony writing. The words he had penned had been wrenched from his heart. He looked forward to spending time with his family, but he was grieved that he would have to share with his beloved Hattie news of an uncertain future. Bounds knew a decision to remain at the *Advocate* would mean the ideals he stood for and the words he penned would utilize the very organization he opposed. The words "You cannot serve two masters" sounded like the bells of the church tower ringing through the countryside. The next morning, as Bounds entered the doors of the publishing house for the last time, he typed out the words of the article he had carried home with him in his coat pocket. It would be his last paper as assistant editor of the *Advocate*, and it came from a broken heart but confident spirit.

LOSS OF CONSCIENCE

It is not a bad thing to have a conscience, that is, to the man intent on doing the right thing in the right way. To him it is a blessing. A conscience enlightened by the Word of God and by His Spirit is like a sun, central and luminous. It guides, warms, and gladdens. A good conscience, trained and sensitive, stands like an ever wakeful guard to protect and warn. Strong and honest convictions are the results of a good conscience. The man of conscience is a reliable man. You know where to find him, and he is worth finding. Conscience may be lost. We can sin against our conscience by violating its injunctions till we not only silence its voice, but destroy its being.

It has been said that papers are spoiled by good-hearted editing, afraid of giving offense. Whether this be true or not, a big lump of good-heartedness, too compliant and presumable, is fatal to a good conscience. There may be much of firmness and much of conscience in a gentle and winning nature, but a soft, yielding will, which does not know its own mind half the time, cannot maintain the vigor native to a good conscience.

Conscience is lost by consulting interest. It knows no debit or credit. It does not belong to the realm of loss or gain. It must do right if the heavens fall, or become bankrupt. Conscience being to duty and to right. It is not for sale—it cannot follow the wrong. Conscience is not a rude boor, neither does it flatter or fawn. It must be true to its convictions without regard to blame or praise. It has but one road—the road of duty and of right. If it loses this road, it loses itself. Conscience has a heart, and must do things heartily.

Insincerity, flattery, mere form, the doing of things by routine is to do them without conscience. The doing of things by routine is perilous to conscience. Habit, when it becomes listless, when it falls into a matter-of-course way of doing things, kills conscience. This getting into the current of great movement, the loss of individuality, the herding with the masses and doing as they do because they do plays havoc with conscience.

It is a matter almost notorious that conscience has gone out of politics, almost out of business, and will not long find a refuge in religion. We cannot banish it in others. Conscience must be cultivated by studying God's will and making his Word the law that directs our actions.

We must look on the moral side of all questions. Conscience is to be cultivated by listening to and obeying its voice. We must cultivate a prayerful, broad, and generous conscience—not a childish, petty, and painfully scrupulous one, which is akin to insincerity more fearful of blame than intent on doing the good and right thing; but a manly conscience, healthy, robust, and resolute. The Christian must have a pure, enlightened conscience; brave, generous, which acts with deliberation and in the fear of God, and supports actions with consistency and firmness. Such consciences are great boons and are

greatly needed. As Cusworht says, "It is the best look-
ing-glass of heaven," knows no fear, dreads no accuser.

We need men in all departments of action and responsibility; in politics, in business, in pew, in pulpit;
who, like Paul, can call God and their consciences as wit-
nesses to every act.

Bounds' article appeared in the *Advocate*, and he
walked the silent valley with a heavy heart. He now felt
his pietistic convictions and life-style were infringed
upon by the church in which he had so lovingly worked.
If he remained an employee, he felt he would be part of
the infraction.

Though he was deeply hurt, he left silently and refused any retirement pay. At fifty-nine years of age, and
with a family to support, Bounds left Nashville and
moved his family to Washington, Georgia, to live with his
father-in-law. It many cases, silence can have a booming
effect. It can produce conviction in the heart and lead to
repentance and restoration for those sensitive to the
Holy Spirit. But this never happened for the church leadership, who never even visited Bounds. They were intent
to remain on the path they had chosen and, therefore,
knew restoration would be impossible with this mighty
prophet.

14

In Exile

I am resting, sweetly resting,
Pillow'd on my Saviour's breast:
In the arms of Jesus cradled,
Sweetly, peacefully I rest;
Trusting in His strength to hold me,
As his blessed arms enfold me,
And in trusting I am blessed.

—Robert O. Smith

When Bounds arrived in Washington, a bustling commerce area in the northeastern section of Georgia, he found a community strong in heritage and culture, with a work ethic typical of the ironlike fiber of the South. Already somewhat familiar with the area because of the months spent there with his in-laws, Bounds was determined to settle his family in and to do what he could to provide well for them.

Very few people in the town maintained themselves out of charity or the government coffers, but Wilkes County supported an agency that provided assistance for any who were needy. These people were referred to as being "on the county." Because the community was tight-knit, when anyone was on the county, it was well-known and carried a certain stigma. If the person was of character and had a desire to earn a living, someone within the county would assist that person with an offer of work. Payment would be either a wage or a barter. Some were sharecroppers, others were hired hands, but most everyone in Wilkes County worked. This included the preachers of that day, many of whom were bivocational pastors. Some of the more affluent churches employed full-time pastors, and most Methodists had a circuit of parishes with which they were involved.

Bounds was one of the few Methodist preachers in his generation to be free to minister in whatever way the Lord led. The bishop of the North Georgia Conference did not assign Bounds to a circuit because Bounds had been released from that obligation. It would be some time before requests and invitations to preach would come his way again.

In his life-style Bounds was a frugal man, but when it came to giving he was generous. He never hesitated to purchase Bibles, tracts, and other literature needed in the evangelization of the heathen. He often sent Bibles to the Methodist missionaries who ministered to the American Indians in the West.

When the Bounds family moved in with the Barnetts in Washington, it may have appeared to others that E. M. was a man of little activity who could not provide for his family. He had not accumulated a large amount of money and would be temporarily dependent on his in-laws. For this reason, people were critical of him and would sometimes shun him. Of course alienating him also provided a convenient way for many to avoid the conviction that came upon them in his presence.

Bounds desired to return to an itinerant ministry. His move from Nashville was strictly on his own, and although he was qualified to receive retirement from the Methodist Church, he never inquired of it or asked for any compensation from the Methodist Episcopal South

Publishing House. Instead, he separated himself from the institution and established himself independently in his wife's hometown.

Bounds was not, however, separating himself from his beloved Methodist Episcopal Church South, and he immediately inquired about a certificate of location from the Missouri Conference. This certificate presented Bounds as a local elder in the church and would allow him to be open for itinerant preaching and teaching. Still, it created a strained relationship between Bounds and the North Georgia Conference bishop, who was already entangled in controversy with evangelist Sam Jones concerning the role of evangelists in the church.

When Bounds left for the National Conference in Memphis, he was sought after by many pastors to speak and preach in the churches and conferences across his denomination. After he resigned his position and moved his family, however, all the notoriety and requests for his presence, counsel, and preaching immediately ceased. One day he was one of the great speakers of the faith in his denomination, and the next it was as though no one had ever heard of him. This rejection was a harsh experience for Bounds.

Many of his former associates and admirers were hesitant to contact him because they were unaware of his reasons for leaving and were unsure how their involvement with him might appear. If it had been a case of immorality, professional compromise, or a spiritual lapse, anyone associated with the situation would come under the scrutiny of others as though they were condoning Bounds in his error. Of course, this was not the case, but because Bounds kept the reasons for his departure to himself many of his friends were hesitant to contact him.

Others stayed away for a different reason. Bounds' stand for absolute integrity within the denomination was spurned by those who aspired to climb the denominational ladder. It could be a detriment to advancement to associate with someone so outspoken. Many in the high positions of the denomination were brought under scrutiny by the ecclesiastical hierarchy regarding their denominational loyalty. Thus, many who were close to Bounds, even at the *Advocate*, felt it necessary to stay away from him for fear of the church's retaliation. Even those who might agree with Bounds in his pietistic stand could not join with him because of the potential blight on their own image. As a result, Bounds found himself in a very lonely and emotionally painful period of his life.

As God allowed His servant and friend to pass through this time of testing, it was as though He were polishing a fine jewel. Even as Bounds experienced disapproval and adversity from the men with whom he had previously enjoyed great fellowship, he remained faithful and determined to be obedient and submissive to almighty God. To be rejected by his friends and co-workers was an experience totally foreign to Bounds—like nothing he had ever encountered in his ministry. Yet, as with the many other tests and trials he had endured, he trusted the Savior and came through the fiery trial with great spiritual review.

In the early part of 1895 Bounds received an invitation from Dr. B. F. Haynes to return to Nashville to take part in a meeting that would be conducted by Rev. C. L. Shelton. Shelton's messages would center on holiness. Here great emphasis would be placed on John Wesley's beliefs related in his book *A Plain Account of Christian Perfection*. This meeting preceded a meeting held in Franklin, Tennessee, on extremism and irrational behavior. Bounds' meeting with Shelton brought about great camaraderie and trust in each other. Their bond of friendship lasted the rest of their days. And Shelton was instrumental many years later in helping to gather Bounds' written materials and putting them into book form.

Bounds would not allow his emotions to override his

call from God. Because he was ostracized by those of his own denomination he made himself available to anyone—any church or group that would call upon him to come and pray, preach, or share. This included a revival of the day called the American Holiness Movement. Because of the movement's pietistic stand, Bounds found himself receiving requests to come and speak in their camp meetings and conferences. He was also sought after by other denominations that were unaware of the situation Bounds faced within his own Methodist Episcopal Church South.

This new avenue of ministry led to his association with many great men of God, such as Dr. Len Broughton of the great Baptist Tabernacle in the heart of Atlanta; A. C. Dixon of Baltimore, Maryland; R. A. Torrey, and a multitude of others from that era.

Bounds' ministry began to flourish once again. God also blessed the Bounds family with the arrival on June 6, 1895, of another daughter, Mary Willis Bounds. Even at the age of sixty, Bounds was excited for this addition to his family and cherished his new daughter.

As summer turned to late fall, the Bounds household was filled with the aroma of holiday meals and treats. Prepared in the quaint kitchen, the smell would permeate the entire house and entice everyone to anticipate the next meal or entertainment of guests. And whenever Bounds returned from preaching or teaching, he brought something in his pocket or case for each child—a symbolic blessing for the faithfulness and love shown their father.

He would continue his afternoon "prayer walks" through this beautiful town, as weather permitted, and pray for the people in each home as he passed.

In February of the following year, just as springtime began to make its first appearance, another flower of beauty was born into the Bounds' home. Her name was Emma. It was a day of celebration in the family and in the community.

In full spring Dr. Leonard G. Broughton and E. M. Bounds arrived in Atlanta for a meeting at the Second Baptist Church. Bounds would make a tremendous impact on this young man, and Dr. Broughton would often use Bounds in his own ministry. The meeting began on a Sunday morning. Almost immediately the services had to be moved from the church into the tabernacle, which had been built for the 1895 campaign of Dr. D. L. Moody. But this building also proved too small, and by the end of the week the meeting had to be moved to a larger space. The meeting continued for several weeks.

As Dr. Len Broughton was about to depart and return to his own church, a delegation from the First Baptist Church asked him to stay another week and preach in their church. Revival broke out there and the meeting continued for several additional weeks. While in the city, Broughton became aware of a small congregation at the Third Baptist Church without a pastor. He was asked if he would consider pastoring this small band of believers "on the wrong side of the tracks." After much prayer and consideration, he accepted the call and began to preach. Within a short period of time, the facilities were outgrown and the congregation had to relocate. Although this occurred in a Southern Baptist Church, the incident would later play a major role in the life of E. M. Bounds.

Despite his being away for many weeks out of every year ministering throughout the countryside, Bounds' relationship with his children was protective and sweet. He penned the following letter to his oldest daughter, Celeste, shortly after her twentieth birthday:

My Precious Celeste,

I should have greeted you on your birthday. But never too late to do good. Time goes by so rapidly. I cannot bring myself to realize that our little Celeste is twenty years old, and if I sometimes treat you as a little child and not as a grown lady it will be that for the time being I have forgotten you are not a child still.

You may be assured the love for the precious child, the darling, has not abated—that I love you and Corneille with a tenderness and sweetness as ever before. Even though you did not draw on me then as you do now, you are more to me than ever before. The memory, image, and loss of your own precious mother has something to do with your endearment to me. I could not have a higher desire for you than that in all things: in purity, simplicity, sweetness, freshness of character, you should be like her. It grieves me much not to have you with me from this time till my happy end on earth shall come and my home indeed shall be reached.

My thoughts go back to your little life in St. Louis. I see you on 12th Street, the crowd of dirty urchins around when you got on the pavement. I can see you before St. Paul's Church with a red balloon in your hand and as the string slipped from your fingers and it went up out of sight how bereft you looked. A greater bereavement, perhaps, in your face than any of the great sorrows of life. I feel satisfied that my precious child is trying to be a Christian, not in name simply, nor in form only, but in deed and truth. Nothing is so empty, vain, delusive as to be a Christian only in name and form. Nothing so satisfying, has such untold riches of hope and joy and peace as to be religious in reality—to love and serve God through Christ by the presence of the Holy Spirit. May you realize, my child, its heavenly riches in this life and in the great life to come. You know that to be a Christian in any saving measure you cannot do as you please, nor enjoy everything you can. The law of your life must be to obey God, and deny self; that heaven is won only by the loss of the world. This life is for God that heaven may be for us. We give this life to God. He gives that life to us.

I was much pleased that in one of your letters you said you were sure all my restraints were intended for your good. Sometimes a rule may work hard and debar us from real pleasure but it saves us often from many a pain. I am sorry now that Corneille rode in a buggy with Mr. Wright. Though her chaperones thought him a fine Christian, he turned out to be so heartless and vain. There are so many vain men who are of good standing and there are other young men whose reputation is not good that I am sure some rules are necessary for parents to shield their girls. It costs me much to restrict you, as much or more than it costs you to be restricted, but no fine young man will ever think the less of you for your obedience to your parents.

I hope you will be spared to me many years to bless my life and that it may please God in His own good time to bring us in a house together here and eventually to our heavenly home, which will be a home indeed.

The 19–21 verses of chap. 8 Romans mean that all the lower creation of God—animals and fruits and flowers and everything has been sadly affected by Adam's sin and that when Christ shall come again they will be benefited by his coming; that man, the lord of creation, will then by the resurrection and its glories be brought into a state of untold liberty from the evils of this life and that the world around us will be wondrously changed into a new heaven and a new earth and the animals and flowers and trees will have a more glorious life. Chap. 12 of Romans is a good one to learn and chap. 35 of Isaiah. If you can get hold of a Methodist hymn book before the last revision of it, learn hymn 620. It is shortened and spoiled in the new hymn book. Number 552 is a noble one, all of it. Some of the hymns on heaven in the new book are good. Learn "Asleep in Jesus."

I cannot tell yet when we can go to Missouri, till I receive some letters. I am a member of the North Georgia Conference, the District Conference elected me to it. It meets at Athens the 24th of this month. If my call to Missouri is not urgent, I will attend that conference before I go.

I am sorry for you to be so far away or even to be away at all, but this is the best opening I see and very valuable to you.

Now, my precious girl, I commend you to God's keeping, God's direction. Make Him your choice. He will direct all your ways. Learn to consult Him in all things and you will be wise and safe in His guidance. I send you a little birthday token. A handkerchief your Aunt Fanny left you . . . keep it as a memorial of her if it will not do to use.

Love to Brother & Sister Haynes, Kiss for Leola & Corneille, Love and Prayers,

Papa

In late June 1898 the entire Bounds family made a trip back to St. Louis to visit his family. His brother Charles had moved to St. Louis several years earlier and was working in the St. Louis Commission and Towing Company on the Mississippi River. He was planning to relocate to Hannibal, and the Bounds family wanted to visit him in St. Louis before the move.

It was a great time of excitement and celebration as the city began its preparations for the 1904 World Fair. The whole family took the old Humbolt trolley out to Forest Park to observe some of the construction that had already begun. Then they returned to Washington, Georgia, relieved to be away from the heat and closeness of city life in St. Louis. Bounds became more accustomed to the quietness of Washington, and found the stress of any big city difficult.

He was still passionate about the subject of true revival, exhibited by this short article published in the *Wesleyan Christian Advocate* on May 10, 1899:

SUPERFICIAL REVIVAL WORK

I have been requested to write concerning superficial revival work. In an age of "sham," when almost every good thing is imitated and the counterfeit is so often palmed off for the genuine, it would be strange if the real work of God in the hearts of men was not substituted by some kind of religion that stopped short of salvation.

There is a religious element that is universal "wherever man is found," and it is a matter of regret that it can be appealed to in such a way as to produce an effect so nearly akin to true religion as to require a keen spiritual discernment to detect the difference between them. So long as man is a sympathetic creature, his sympathies can be so wrought upon as to bring him credit for a spirituality to which he is an entire stranger; and so long as he is emotional, his spasmodic gushes of feeling may be mistaken for the manifestations of a truly penitent soul, or for the indisputable signs of one brought from under the yoke of the bondage of sin. A preacher who delights to "dwell among the tombs," and whose sermons consist largely in descriptions of deathbed scenes, may even go so far as to melt his hearers to tears, or to lift them, in imagination at least, to the third heaven, and yet leave the great depths of the soul undisturbed, or if he is a singer, he may so render "Beckoning Hands" as to attract the attention to the hands of spirits beckoning to realms of light, while the too worn, empty, weary, and appealing hands of many of the sons of men are lost sight of.

It is quite common for the standing up for prayer and card signing methods of carrying on revivals to be made light of, but much of the altar work, as we see it these days, is hardly better. After a sympathetic sermon has been preached, penitents are invited to the altar; and too often incompetent and inexperienced church members are invited to talk to them. If the poor souls have any conviction to begin with, they are too often talked out of it before they leave. A few remarks like the following are made: "Jesus loves you." "He died for sinners." "Don't you think He died for you?" "Then he is your Savior, isn't He?" "Now, don't you believe He saves you?" The truth is, the poor creature has not even apprehended the "exceeding sinfulness of sin," and has never met the conditions that must *necessarily* be met before one can possibly *believe* "even unto the saving of the soul." The "right eye" sin is not plucked out, nor is the "right hand" sin cut off; he has not paid the *cost* of discipleship—that of forsaking all and following the Christ. He possibly weeps some, makes some good resolutions, either of which has the effect of making him feel better, and this good feeling is mistaken for the new birth and he is pronounced a child of God, when as yet he is still in the "gall of bitterness and the bonds of iniquity." A full surrender is not easily made. Giving up all sin and all love of the world costs an effort which few are willing to make.

The evangelist who preaches for eternity is never great on numbers. He is not apt to count hundreds of converts where there is no restitution, no confession, and no glad cry which proclaims, "The lost is found, the dead is made alive again!" The man who must meet God in the judgment to have his work tried by fire cannot afford to work on superficial lines, and to cry, "Peace, peace, when there is no peace." To be an empiric when it comes to treating the ills of the body is bad enough, but to be a "quack" in dealing with the souls of men is infinitely worse.

Let each one of us as preachers be as was the fabled lioness who when twitted that she had but one cub answered, "True, but he is a *lion*." It is far better that we have one soul, truly saved, than a hundred vain professions of salvation from those who give no satisfactory evidence that they have indeed "passed from death unto life."

In the summer of 1900 a great sorrow encompassed their serene little town. A dispute had broken out between John Levingood and Dillard Handon. The dispute was insignificant but the outcome was tragic. Handon killed Levingood. A man of faith, Handon had been pushed to the point of lashing out in anger and then took the life of the other. He was found guilty and sentenced to be hanged. August 17 was the day of execution. He called for Bounds and F. B. Barnett. They both went to the jail, shared the Word of God, and gained the assurance of Handon's salvation. Then, along with Sheriff Joshua B. Goodwin, they knelt in the cell and prayed together. Afterward they all stood and sang "What a Friend We Have in Jesus." Dillard Handon was led to the gallows. A fleeting moment, unguarded and unprotected, had allowed his emotions to control his body, and now he too would die. This was a difficult time for Bounds and Barnett to have to walk the line between compassion and judgment. Ultimately the penalty of sin was paid for by Jesus Christ. But the consequences of the sin of murder, in this case, was paid for by Dillard Handon.

As the year came to a close, Brother Bounds meditated upon its accomplishments. He thought about his beloved church and about evangelism across the nation, and a burden swelled in his heart; a fire burned in his bosom. All the major denominations had made special efforts to sweep in the twentieth century. Programs, banners, slogans, and well-meaning events had been planned. Some believed the year would bring the return of Christ. Others believed the world would be evangelized. Yet at its conclusion, neither had come to pass. In most of the major Christian periodicals there seemed to be silence with regard to the unfulfilled hopes, dreams, and aspirations of this year of jubilee. Though much effort and money was expended, little or no spiritual benefit emerged. Or so it seemed.

But Brother Bounds began to hear small reports of spiritual revival in certain churches. The churches were primarily small and insignificant by the denomination's standards yet open and available to God's standard of holiness. A small dewdrop of revival seemed to be emerging in these obscure locations. So as the new century dawned, it was with great expectation that Brother Bounds looked to the future.

15

The New Century

A ministry may be a very thoughtful ministry without prayer; the preacher may secure fame and popularity without prayer; the whole machinery of the preacher's life and work may be run without the oil of prayer . . . but no ministry can be a spiritual one, securing holiness in the preacher and in his people without prayer being made an evident and controlling force.

—E. M. Bounds

The year 1901 began with very little commotion in the community. However, exciting things were building in the Bounds family. June saw the weddings of two of their daughters—Celeste and Corneille. They were married in a double wedding ceremony on June 20. It was performed by the brides' father, E. M. Bounds, and assisted by their mother's brother, Rev. Frank W. Barnett. It was a grand celebration that had the whole town talking.

After the death of President McKinley in September, a special service was held in the Methodist church that included all of the community. They came together to worship and to mourn their president. Bounds led in prayer during the memorial service.

E. M. Bounds began his days at home with prayer. He would rise at four and usually pray until seven. Then he

133

would join his family for breakfast. Afterward he would spend a time of prayer and worship with the family before returning to his own prayer chamber. This was a special place on the second floor of his home. He developed the habit of writing paragraphs on slips of paper. These were words saturated with prayer, coming from a heart of prayer, on the subject of prayer. Soon the notes became volumes of untold wealth.

During this time, the Third Baptist Church of Atlanta had outgrown their building under the anointed leadership of Dr. Broughton. He had a great vision to duplicate the D. L. Moody Bible Conferences he had attended in years past and to introduce this type of conference to the South. So he began to build a new wooden tabernacle in the heart of Atlanta.

A year later Bounds received an invitation to speak at the first of these Atlanta Baptist Tabernacle Conferences. This time he took his son Osborne along. Bags in hand, they boarded a train headed west. As the conductor approached the pair, he inquired of their destination. Bounds said, "My son and I are going to Atlanta." With that he withdrew from his pocket a handful of change and said, "I know this is not enough to get us all the way to our destination, but you can put us off at the point where this fare runs out."

The conductor quickly counted the coins and said, "Brother Bounds, this is not nearly enough to get you and the boy there. I would have to put you off in the middle of a field somewhere." Bounds replied, "Well, if we are put out in the middle of a field, it will be precisely where God wants us to be."

As a young man, Osborne was impressed by his father's trust and faith in God. When the conductor walked away, a well-groomed businessman approached the pair and said, "I understand you are Reverend Bounds, and that you and the boy don't have quite enough to get to your destination."

"So we are told," Bounds answered.

The businessman quickly enjoined, "Well, your fare is covered, Brother Bounds. Have a blessed meeting in Atlanta."

It was from meetings such as these that many personal contacts would be developed into long-lasting and eternal friendships. And it was here, three years later, that Bounds would meet Dr. Homer Hodge, who would be influential in compiling and editing the entire works of E. M. Bounds. Others he would meet and influence were individuals such as W. E. Blackstone, A. C. Dixon, S. D. Gordon, R. A. Torrey, Arthur T. Pierson, Samuel Chadwick, F. B. Meyer, and Dr. G. Campbell Morgan. He would also be able, once again, to fellowship with his close evangelist friend, Sam Jones.

In November he became a grandfather, when Celeste gave birth to a daughter and named her Emma. This was a glorious time for Bounds and he delighted in the precious gift bestowed upon the family. (Emma eventually would marry a missionary and go to the foreign field. Later she would return to Atlanta and serve as a professor at Emory University.)

On June 19, 1903, a second grandchild was presented to Brother Bounds. Corneille gave him a grandson called Edward Barnett. This was a special and happy occasion in the life of the whole Bounds family.

And on June 6, 1904 (the same birthdate as Bounds' youngest daughter), Celeste bore a fine baby boy named Fielding Hill.

Soon the calls to preach that Brother Bounds received from around the nation took on a new dimension. Few knew of him in the North Georgia Conference, so he began networking to become friends with and establish his credibility among these brethren. They soon realized that he was an extraordinary man of high integrity, who had great insight not only into the church itself but into the structure of many denominations. They witnessed his close following of John Wesley's teaching and his adherence to the Word of God and its authority. His strong stance and piety was evident through his declaration, yet he never condemned or spoke condescendingly to anyone. He held the standard of holiness with dignity and with great love and compassion for everyone.

Throughout the next two years a spiritual awakening began to sweep the countryside, even crossing the ocean to the country of Wales, where a young evangelist named Seth Joshua preached holiness throughout the region. Evan Roberts, inspired by Joshua's burning spirit, returned home to Gorseinon, and to his home church, Libanus. On October 31, 1904, a great revival began there that circled the globe—touching lives, churches, denominations, and every fiber of society with a mighty force. This great movement of God became known as the Spiritual Awakening. (Also known as the Great Awakening.)

In the early spring of 1905 Bounds received an invitation to come to Elberton, Georgia, to conduct a meeting with Clement C. Cary, another pietistic Methodist with a clear vision for traditional Methodism and a prophetic eye looking toward the future. The meeting enjoyed much spiritual success. The town became a bustling outpouring of a spirit of excitement as this great man of God, so humbly and without fanfare, came and shared the Word of God with the people under an anointing that was very evident in his life. He aroused the churches and the town to a renewed interest in spiritual matters. The atmosphere became charged with the acknowledgment of a holy and divine God, and many people affiliated themselves with the church as they embraced the loving and saving Lord Jesus.

In May a group of preachers arrived at Broughton's

Atlanta Baptist Tabernacle Conference a few days early. Several of them had come from various parts of the world for this great meeting. Much talk and consideration was given to the revival, and people were excited to be able to come to the conference and share what God was doing in their area as well as across the nation and in the world. This was one of the largest conferences ever held at the Atlanta Baptist Tabernacle.

It was this spring meeting that saw a local Atlanta pastor, Homer Werle Hodge, introduced to E. M. Bounds. Hodge was seeking a deeper understanding of the ways of God, and many recommended he seek out the fellowship of Bounds. This proved to be orchestrated by the hand of God because from this meeting came many of the volumes of books penned by Bounds; edited and readied for printing through the efforts of Homer Hodge. They would share close fellowship together for the rest of Bounds' days. Hodge had this to say of the meeting:

> When I met this great saint in May 1905 he was seventy years old. He was then writing his *Preacher and Prayer*, along with his thoughts on the Resurrection. We shared board and bed often until his death. It was worth much to hear him talk. He would sit for hours in silent meditation and prayer and then begin in a delightful sweet way. If we broke in upon him he became very intense. To understand his meaning and his earnestness at times was painful. He coaxed us to rise with him at 4:00 A.M. and wrestle for the lost world and for money to publish his books. At last God gave him the loan of money enough to publish *Preacher and Prayer*, and *Resurrection* in 1907. The two books were written (figuratively speaking) in his blood and saturated through with his tears.

The Preacher and Prayer, begun in 1905 and published in 1907, was the result of Bounds' notes on insights on prayer and information gathered from the revivals. As he recalled and meditated upon the great spiritual movements of God and made observations as a student of the Word of God and of John Wesley, he found weaknesses in the experiences that were coming out of the meetings of 1904–1905. Revival and spiritual awakenings often assault the emotions of people. For this reason, Bounds felt that a foundation of biblical doctrine must be taught to the new converts. Otherwise, they would begin their spiritual walk seeking additional experiences rather than seeking God. The great influx of converts into the churches during the 1904–1905 Awakening was a phenomenon to experience and study. But the effect of the revival dissipated rapidly among the newly converted. Those who were already Christians developed a deeper walk and a greater understanding of the ways of God, but they were negligent in sharing it effectively with the new disciples.

In particular, Bounds noticed a deficiency in the activities of the church with regard to prayer. People were praying for the lost but they expected the lost to come to the church rather than personally seeking them out. Because there was a true spiritual awakening the general atmosphere was permeated with an awareness of God, and often people *would* come to church seeking release from the conviction of the Holy Spirit. But Bounds taught that it is always the ministry of the church to go into the highways and byways and compel sinners to come in and to share the Good News with them where they live.

Bounds was well aware that after a true revival the question always comes: "Now what?" He also knew that prayer must be an intimate experience with a holy God, one that so influences a person's life as to make him willing to lay aside his reliance on the four walls of a church building and carry his spiritual walk into the pagan pool to share the glories of God with others. This process begins by full submission to God in the closet of prayer as one stands spiritually naked before God inquiring of His leadership and direction for life.

After the Great Awakening, it was apparent that people tended to look after experiences rather than walking by faith because prayers were directed toward the needs or desires of the church and not toward the reaching of the lost. Worship started to evolve in the direction of the four gods: "I," "me," "my," and "mine." Bounds was driven by an internal passion to share the importance of intimate prayer with a holy God. With this message he focused his attention toward the preachers, seeking to inspire them to make God preeminent in their lives.

Bounds believed and lived the premise that if a Christian in holy communion with almighty God focuses on God rather than on prayer and experience, sin will become so repugnant to him that he cannot return to it. Also, when his focus is upon God and His exaltation, God will direct his path in the way of righteousness, service, and ministry. Bounds also felt that if God expected His children to do only what they were naturally capable of doing, they would do it in their own strength. When the focus is on God, He directs our path in what we can do by faith.

As the revival ebbed in 1905, many churches focused on activities directed toward self rather than submission to God. Forum and programs became the hallmark of the day instead of submission, obedience, and sacrifice. Church leadership began to try to emulate what God had done through the Great Awakening and to duplicate the experiences. Yet they were unable to duplicate the movement of the Spirit of almighty God. Bounds challenged Christians to the command of Christ to "seek first the kingdom of God and His righteousness." The will of God is not geographical but positional. Standing "holy and acceptable before God is our reasonable service" and is the perfect will of God for our lives. Otherwise, church "activities" will be just that rather than the result of fresh anointing and empowerment.

It was at one of the meetings at Atlanta Baptist Tabernacle that Bounds was again encouraged to put his writings together in the form of a book. He met Dr. G. Campbell Morgan from London, and shared with him parts of the manuscript. Dr. Morgan encouraged Bounds to finish the work and come to London and acquire a publisher.

As 1905 was drawing to an close, little Edward, Corneille's son named for Bounds, became very ill. The child continued to worsen, and on November 5 he died. He was laid to rest in the Bounds plot in Washington, Georgia. To lose a grandchild, especially one named for him, was a devastating blow to Bounds. Sorrow and grief would visit the family again in the spring with the loss of Hattie's mother, Elizabeth Barnett. During these months Bounds continued to write and pray as never before.

In 1907, manuscript in hand, Bounds went to London to present his work to the editors of Marshall Brothers. In the same year they would publish E. M. Bounds' first book, *The Preacher and Prayer*. Shortly thereafter, the publishing house of the Methodist Episcopal Church South, in the United States, also printed a version of this masterpiece. It was a great victory for Bounds to be able to present to the church his work in print.

The next summer Bounds' brother Charles died. He was laid to rest beside his wife at the Mt. Olive Cemetery in Hannibal. It was both sad and ironic that the Bounds family, so close in life, would be buried so far from one another. His father, in Shelbyville; his mother, in Kirksville; and now Charles, in Hannibal. But of course their eternal destiny was exactly the same.

Rev. Robert O. Smith asked Bounds to hold a meeting for him in December of 1911 at their small church in Winterhaven, a few miles east of Athens, Georgia. Bounds had last conducted a revival for Smith in 1899. By now Bounds was quite elderly and dealing with profound reflections in his ministry. He wanted to share his vision of the necessity of prophets—men of God to draw the people in the church back to God through repentance and submission. The churches in America were getting away from the foundational truths—the indwelling Spirit of God, submission to the lordship of Christ, and the inerrancy of the Word of God. Without prophets anchored in these truths, the church drifts, blowing to and fro with the winds of the whims and fancies of man.

Smith recognized that this might be his last opportunity to have the great patriarch Dr. E. M. Bounds in his pulpit. He was spellbound by his assessment of how the prophets of God had been neglected and, further, how that neglect was as deadly as any element opposing the ways of God.

In 1912 Bounds submitted an article to the *Wesleyan Advocate* that had a great impact on its subscribers. It came out a few months before his death:

KILLING THE PROPHETS

It certainly does seem strange that notwithstanding the scarcity of true prophets, everywhere so many persist in putting them to death. But prophet-killers are as truly in the world today as they have ever been in any age of the world—as truly as prophets themselves are in the world. It is true that prophets are seldom killed as they were in former years, but they are being killed and that beyond the possibility of resurrection.

First of all, prophets are too often killed in the colleges and, alas, not seldom in those institutions of learning known as Christian colleges.

Fortunate indeed is the young man who can be filled

up with some men's notions of theology, biology, psychology, and the like and escape with an unshaken confidence in the biblical history of man, the certainty of Divine revelation, the supernaturalism in regeneration, and the fundamentals of "Holy Writ."

Too little regard is paid to the selections of those who, of all men, should be "sound in the faith" and "filled with the Spirit." No man can properly teach others who is not himself born and taught of God.

Then, too, the prophet is often killed by flattery. That principle in the heart that loves the praise of men rather than being content with the approval of God is pampered and fed until the prophet is slain, while as yet his inexperienced feet stand upon the threshold of what would otherwise prove a life of great service. Inflated by the glittering compliments of the unwise, he attempts to soar, but only like Lucifer, the Son of the morning, to fall, and only God knows "how great is that fall."

But if flattery fails to destroy the prophet, his love of money is strongly appealed to. . . . A reasonable salary will not suffice. Foodstuffs have advanced, and clothing, especially clothing, is unreasonably high. The prophet and his family must keep up with the procession, even if they do not lead it. Something must be done; soft clothing and long robes—these must be had at any cost. Money, not faith, must answer the questions "What must I eat? What must I drink or Wherewithal shall I be clothed?"

Then, again, the prophet is sometimes killed by the abuse and persecutions of those to whom he preaches; beaten with many stripes, starved out, and frozen out by heartless professors, he occasionally turns from his thankless hearers and seeks the shade of some juniper tree, where he becomes the easy victim of some prophet of Baal who teaches him to compromise the truth, to keep back "his sword from blood," and to cry, "peace, peace, when there is no peace." And now, if he be not carried away into the maelstrom of secular life, he perhaps receives the call to some city pulpit, where the majestic tones of the organ have swallowed up the mutterings of Sinai; and where it may be truthfully said of him, he is dead while he liveth.

Don't kill the prophets. We need them. True prophets, men of God; men mighty in prayer and in the Scriptures. They may sometimes be unlettered men, as were Peter, James, John, and a host of others; they may be rugged men, and so many of them are, but the light is on their brow, the fire in their eye, the message of God on their lips. Theirs is the heavenly armor. They have the sword of the Spirit and courageously do they wield it! I say again, don't kill the prophets, these men who lie upon their faces and commune with God until their countenances shine as did the face of Moses, and their garments smell of frankincense and myrrh. Don't slay the prophets, lest God destroy thee with the "breath of his nostrils, when his wrath is kindled but a little."

16

His Journey Ends

Go aside, beloved, and rest awhile;
Well hast thou borne the burdens of life's day,
And thou hast rescued sinners poor and vile,
Till worn and old, then rest awhile, we pray.
Thou hast not sought the honors Earth can give,
Nor deigned to hoard her vain delusive pelf,
But for her richer weal was wont to give
Thy manhood's strength, and sacrifice thyself.
Now go aside and rest, nor faintly dream
Thy work hath been in vain, nor shed one tear;
Brother, behold among the crowns that gleam
With shining gems—thy crown awaits thee where
Christ's soldiers never feel the hand of time,
Where wintry age no more shall ever come,
Out of earth's frost and chill, into a clime
Where youth immortal blooms—behold thy home!

—Robert O. Smith

As the spring of 1912 began to wane into summer, the azaleas displayed their lovely blossoms and the dogwoods dropped their petals of pure white. Bounds, at the age seventy-six, was invited to take part in a celebration of dedication, which he always enjoyed immensely. In the northwest area of Wilkes County, the Hills Chapel Methodist Church was to be dedicated.

On July 7 Brother Bounds, with Dr. James E. Pickui, preached a message of dedication and vision to the church. The young pastor, W. A. Woodruff, was elated to have Brother Bounds in this service. He and others sensed this was a great day but were unaware that this would be the last formal proclamation Bounds would make. Here he would deliver his last message to the church.

As the summer heat began to dissipate, Bounds continued his ministry of prayer and writing. And as people all around began to read *The Preacher and Prayer*, an even greater interest in him and his teaching emerged. In turn, interest began to stir for the Methodist Episcopal Church South. At the St. Louis Conference in mid-September, J. R. Vaughn would share a paper from the overflow of his love and admiration for this great patriarch and friend:

Yet his preaching did not inspire the multitudes. Not even the ordinary church would long wait on his ministry. They thought his standard impossible—too unworldly—though they confessed it was scriptural. Hence, he preached for the few—to those who would be spiritual leaders, and so preserve the standard of "deeper yet" in a generation too content with half-measures in religion.

He knew the circle he reached was limited for the time, but they would carry the testimony to the wider circles; and he had faith to wait.

He was without ambition for honors. In any form they were distasteful. When unknown and undesired by him, the degree of D.D. was conferred upon him, he was embarrassed that he must carry the title all of his days.

But Brother Bounds was preeminently a man of prayer. Not without reason has he been styled the David Brainerd of Southern Methodism. He preached on prayer and, above all, he practiced prayer. He studied

Brainerd's diary, absorbed his spirit, and rewrote for publication a history of this eminent saint. His little book *The Preacher and Prayer* is a gem of terse discussion and rousing exhortation on this subject. I have never known one to read it who was not stirred by it. Here again, he speaks to the few. He aims at the vital circle. He believes that the minister holds the key to holy living and power in the church. If he could reach them, they would reach the church. The church will not live higher than the pastor prays. The prayers of this godly man have sent this book out as a herald to its mark. . . .

After *The Preacher and Prayer* began to have an impact, Bounds again addressed one of the weaknesses of the revivals and personal prayer life. He began "The Great While Before Day Prayer Bands," a system of accountability for people growing in their prayer life, which has recently gained renewed popularity.

At the end of 1912 and in early 1913 Bounds continued meeting with Dr. Hodge with regard to the printing of additional materials that had accumulated through his latter years. Much of his writing told of the need for accountability among the people who pray, along with the need of emphasis on the prayer closet experience. Jesus gave a command when He said, "When thou prayest, enter into thy closet, and when thou hast shut thy door. . . ." It sets the foundation for intimacy with a holy God that is the prerequisite for sustaining a viable and vibrant prayer life. Until individuals develop a close, loving relationship with God through prayer, they will be unable to truly know God and walk in the admonition that He desires of them.

Bounds continued to be assured that his writings would be put into book form and published. This mantle fell primarily to the intellect and discernment of the humble Claudius Chilton, aided and encouraged by Robert O. Smith, Clement C. Cary, and finally implemented by Homer W. Hodge. To these men fell the task of securing, editing, and compiling the remaining books that carried the name of E. M. Bounds as their author. It would be appropriate to receive from these men and others of that day words of description and testimony of Dr. Bounds.

Dr. Hodge became the primary force to take the edited work and see it into printed form. In the introduction to the book *Prayer and Praying Men* (Baker Book House), Dr. Hodge shares his heart in reflection of the impact Brother Bounds had on his life with the following words:

> Rev. Edward McKendree Bounds was passionately devoted to his beloved Lord and Savior Jesus Christ. His devotion was extraordinary in that he was praying and writing about Him all the time, except during the hours of sleeping.
>
> God gave Bounds a largeness of heart and an insatiable desire to do service for Him. To this end he enjoyed what I am pleased to term a transcendent inspiration, else he could never have brought out of his treasury things new and old far exceeding anything we have known or read.
>
> Bounds is easily the Betelguese of the devotional sky. There is no man that has lived since the days of the apostles that has surpassed him in the depths of his marvelous research into the life of prayer.
>
> He was busily engaged in writing on his manuscripts when the Lord said unto him, "Well done, thou good and faithful servant, enter thou into the joy of thy Lord."
>
> Wesley was of the sweetest and most forgiving disposition, but when aroused he was a man of the "keenest penetration with a gift of speech that bit like the stroke of a whip." Bounds was meek and humble, and never did we know him to retaliate upon any of his enemies. He cried over them and wept, praying for them early and late.
>
> Wesley was easily gulled. "My brother," said Charles,

on one occasion in disgusting accents, "was, I believe, born for the benefit of knaves." No man could impose on Bounds' credulity. He was a diagnostician of rare ability. Bounds shied away from all frauds in profession and would waste no time upon them.

Wesley was preaching and riding all day. Bounds was praying and writing day and night.

Wesley would not allow any misrepresentations of his doctrinal positions in his later years. Bounds was in this respect very much like him.

Wesley came to his fame while yet alive. He was always in the public eye. Bounds, while editing a *Christian Advocate* for twelve years, was little known out of his church.

Wesley, at eighty-six, could still preach on the streets for thirty minutes. Bounds was able at seventy-five in the first hour of the fourth watch to pray for three hours upon his knees.

Wesley, at the time of his death, had enjoyed fifty-six years of preferment. His name was on every tongue. Christianity was born again in England under his mighty preaching and organization. Bounds was comparatively unknown for fifty years, but will recover the "lost and forgotten secret of the church" in the next fifty years.

Wesley's piety and genius and popularity flowed from his early life like a majestic river. Bounds' has been dammed up, but now is beginning to sweep with resistless force and ere long he will be the mighty Amazon of the devotional world.

Henry Crabbe Robinson said in his diary when he heard Wesley preach at Colchester, "He stood in a wide pulpit and on each side of him stood a minister, and the two held him up. His voice was feeble and he could hardly be heard, but his reverent countenance, especially his long white locks, formed a picture never to be forgotten." Rev. E. M. Bounds, just ten months before his death, preached with his voice feeble and his sentences run together. His sermon was only twenty minutes long, when he quietly came to the end and seemed exhausted.

Wesley had sufficient money and to spare during all his career. Bounds did not care for money. He did not depreciate it; he considered it the lowest order of power.

Wesley died with "an eye beaming and lips breaking into praise." "The best of all is God with us," Bounds wrote. "When He is ready I am ready; I long to taste the joys of the heavenlies."

Wesley said, "The world is my parish." Bounds prayed as if the universe was his zone.

Wesley was the incarnation of unworldliness, the embodiment of magnanimity. Bounds was the incarnation of unearthliness, humility, and self-denial. Wesley will live in the hearts of saints for everlasting ages. Bounds eternally.

Wesley sleeps in the City Road Chapel grounds, among his "bonny dead," under marble, with fitting tribute chiseled in prose, awaiting the resurrection. Bounds sleeps in the Washington, Georgia Cemetery, without marble covering, awaiting the Bridegroom's coming.

These two men held ideals high and clear beyond the reach of other men. Has this race of men entirely gone out of the world now that they are dead?

Ultimately E. M. Bounds' time on this earth came to a close. The *Nashville Christian Advocate* published the following notice:

Rev. E. M. Bounds, D.D., long prominent in the ministry of our church, died August 24, 1913, at his home in Washington, Georgia, aged seventy-eight years. Dr. Bounds spent a good number of years in Missouri, where his ministry was a most successful one, and in many other states where he labored his ministry was blessed of the Lord to the saving of many. For some time he was Assistant Editor of the *Christian Advocate*, serving in that capacity with Bishop E. E. Hoss. For fifteen years he had made his home in Washington, Georgia.

The Church loses a faithful minister and a man honored because of his life of genuine consecration to his Lord's service. His wife and seven children survive him. Many friends throughout Southern Methodism sorrow with them.

Though this great man of God wrote books that had been published by this agency and were among their bestselling books, this was the only comment of his life's achievement. It was recorded in a few short lines of the newspaper to which he gave so much of his life. But Bounds would not have desired any more; instead, it was his desire that the books he wrote out of the overflow of his love for God would go forth as wings of eagles to lift the despairing of the world; to strengthen the saints and to bend their knees to intercede and weep for the lost and dying peoples of the world. His great desire was to be found pleasing to the Lord.

From the foreword of the book *The Possibilities of Prayer* (Baker Book House), and from a later article in the *Herald of Holiness*, Dr. B. S. Haynes, who was converted under Brother Bounds' ministry and later became the managing editor of the *Tennessee Advocate* and the third president of Asbury College, penned these words:

Our first sight of this great saint was at the close of the Civil War, when he was dropped into our village in Tennessee with his uniform on. We remember how our childish minds were particularly taken with the gray jeans jacket, closely buttoned with its brilliant brass buttons. He took charge of our little Methodist Church. We remember with what soul-stirring pathos and fervor he read those old classic hymns, such as "Majestic Sweetness Sits Enthroned," "How Sweet the Name of Jesus Sounds," "In Evil Long I Took Delight," and many others. Often, when our childish feet would near the church door, the hope would involuntarily arise in our minds that he would read one of those wonderful hymns we had heard him read before. Always he broke our young hearts by the inimitably seraphic way of his reading of the opening hymn before he preached the sermon. And the sermon! Who can describe it? Simple, direct, soulful, it went where it was invariably aimed—to the heart of the hearer.

The form of this holy, diminutive man, lying prone with a heavenly smile on his face, while his voice shouted the praises of God in the humble village prayer meeting, is a sweet and familiar picture in our childhood's memory.

Great in native intellect, great in spiritual insight, great in reading the Gospel from hymn or God's Word, great with his pen and greater in prevailing prayer to his Father-God, great as a father, friend, husband, and counselor, great in simple faith, dauntless adherence to the right and truth and God; greatest of all in humility, uncomplaining, submission, and in intercession, Dr. Bounds lived comparatively unknown for what he really was. But his works will follow him, and we believe his posthumous fame will grow with the years, and though dead he will continue to speak in broader lines and larger visible results than during life. . . .

This man of God has passed to his eternal reward. We have no words to express our sense of personal bereavement. He was our pastor in childhood, the first we remember to have known; he was our spiritual father, our conversion occurring at fourteen years of age; he has been our sincere friend and spiritual monitor during all the years that have elapsed since we first met him in the dawn of young life; he has been our inspiration in life's struggle and conflicts—a wise advisor and friend in crisis, a comfort in time of trouble, a constant and faithful inciter to higher and nobler attainments in grace, all along the changeful years of the checkered past.

Dr. Bounds was a marvelous combination. The very embodiment of profound humility, he was a hero, a Spartan, a Napoleon of calm and dauntless courage. Meek and self-depreciative to a point painful to his most intimate friends, he was yet one of the best and most widely read men we ever knew, and wielded a fragile and trenchant pen distinguished alike in forensic defense of the truth and in the mysteries and glories of the depths of prayer and the deeper spiritual things of life.

He became entirely too religious and too intensely spiritual for his church. The time came when he could no longer consistently and with a clear conscience accept work at the hand of the authorities of his church. So he quietly retired to his humble home in a Georgian village, without saying as much in explanation of his retirement inculpatory of his church as we have said above. During these long and lonely years he has lived in his books and on his knees. At four o'clock (A.M.) daily he was found on his knees agonizing with God for friend and foe in tears and intensity of earnestness. Then twice or thrice daily afterward he was at the same business of praying. And with him it was a BUSINESS. This was what he was pleased to call praying. It was the Christian's great business. Saturated constantly thus with the spirit of prayer and surcharged with the very oxygen of heaven, he pored over his books or delved with his pen.

In 1891, when the holiness revival had come to the writer's city and many of us had crossed over into Canaan, Dr. Bounds was at one time a visitor during a great holiness meeting and the guest of the leader of the movement. One morning this leader came into our editorial office, and addressing us familiarly said, "Haynes, your man Bounds is a queer sort of fellow. This morning long before day, I was awakened by an unusual noise like earnest, if not controversial talking. It bothered me. I listened, and it seemed to be in or near by guest chamber, where Dr. Bounds was sleeping. Listening more intently, I caught his words and heard my name called, followed by his earnest entreaty for me, as if I were in great danger and he was pleading for me. I listened from a little nearer position, and was dumbfounded to find he was in a great agony of prayer and tears for my soul and was pleading with God to awaken me to my real situation and to lead me out into a larger place. He talked just like he believed I was a backslider or a hypocrite." This brother was in trouble. I told him he had better look narrowly within, for Bounds was one of the truest and most remorseless spiritual diagnosticians I had ever met; that he had camped on my trail for thirty years, and really had been the chief means of prodding me up and keeping me in line. . . .

Immersed in my labors, and letting my correspondence lag for long months at a time, often I have been summarily aroused by something like this: "Don't get too busy to pray. Praying is your greatest, your chief business, and there is no substitute for it."

Another editorial on September 14, 1927, by Rev. C. F. Winberly, D.D., revealed his perception of Bounds as he excerpted an article called "Modern Apostle of Faith":

A story of continuity: David Brainerd, a missionary to the American Indians, kept a diary. After his death, Jonathan Edwards published it; William Carey, a humble shoemaker read it and went to India; Henry Martyn read it and went to Persia; McCheyne read it and went to the Jews; E. M. Bounds read it and went to his knees. He remained there until he solved the problem of intercessory prayer to a degree without parallel in the history of Methodism. On that particular night, no lights shown in the little village except the flickering street lights. But one other light glimmered through the shutters into the spacious enclosure of an old southern home. But the light was not all that shone there, it was indeed dim compared to the vision of the man who was now preparing for the work of the day. Shortly after four o'clock, the watchers at Heaven's outposts flashed the message to headquarters: "Behold, he prayeth."

The vision was that of a practical mystic—a man of

piercing black eyes, slight, spare figure. As he kneeled, it was no mere whisper in which the prayer was breathed. Edward M. Bounds believed and practiced audible supplication. Perhaps few think it matters in what voice we pray. Few think to pray in a voice that moves. Dr. Bounds' praying voice possessed a confidence, an earnest assurance we have never heard reproduced. Dr. Bounds did not merely pray well that he might write well about prayer; he prayed because the needs of the world were upon him. He prayed for long years upon subjects to which the easy-going Christian rarely gives a thought. He prayed for objects which men of less faith are always ready to call impossible. Yet from these continued solitary prayer-vigils, year by year, there arose a gift of prayer-teaching equaled by few men in history. He wrote transcendently about prayer, because he was transcendent in its practice.

With the arrival of Edward McKendree Bounds, born within the little log cabin on the Salt River in the heartland of Missouri, the world would never be the same. When that small voice cried out for the first time in that little cabin, the populace of the world had no idea of the magnificent work that God would perform through this man.

Seventy-eight years later, in a majestic home in the heart of Washington, Georgia, in a room saturated with love and admiration, that voice became silent. The frail, weak, trembling hands that had penned the richness of his heart stopped trembling. The lips that told of the blessing of sweet communion and holy intercourse with God now quieted as they surrendered life in this body of clay to a new life in the presence of the Lord. In the peacefulness of evening, this spiritual giant, Brother E. M. Bounds, very quietly and with a serenity of godliness slipped into the arms of his loving Savior, Jesus Christ.

Acknowledgments

It has been twenty years of gathering information, scraps of paper, dates, names, interviews, recordings, photos; traveling from the archives in our national capitol to the backwoods and back roads of Missouri; from the historical towns of Hannibal, Missouri, to Washington, Georgia, and into the big cities of St. Louis, Nashville, Vicksburg, and Atlanta; of going to the state capitols and searching through the documentation of the Bounds families from Mobile to Nashville, to Columbia, Missouri.

To footnote every item recorded in this volume would require a matching volume and be most impractical. Instead, I have decided to make the historical accounting of this book available upon request. If a reader of this volume has questions with regard to events in the life of E. M. Bounds and/or the information therein, I would be happy to respond to any legitimate request.

I realize that many individuals have studied the writings of Bounds and that Baker Book House has diligently served in producing the volumes and classics of Bounds throughout the years. Though many have been printed and reprinted several times, there are still those studying the writings of Bounds for the first time. In 1993 two volumes—*Prayer and Revival* and *Powerful and Prayer-*

ful Pulpits—came from the research that I have done in acquiring editorials that Bounds penned at the *Nashville Advocate*. Both of these books are available through Baker Book House. Additional editorials are available through the E. M. Bounds School of Prayer.

I would like to thank Bethany House Publishers and my editor, Steve Laube, for ushering this volume into print.

Listed below are those who have diligently helped in securing specific information and have been most generous in encouragement and research. Even as they are listed, I realize that there are some that will be missed. To those, I humbly beg forgiveness, realizing that all of our work has come to provide this volume, and our efforts have not been in vain but will give an accounting of what God has done through E. M. Bounds.

A. B. Church, Jr., Franklin, Tennessee
Alabama Historical Society, Birmingham, Alabama
Alan Farley, Appomattox, Virginia
Barbour County Courthouse, Clayton, Alabama
Carter House Center, Franklin, Tennessee
Dallas County Courthouse, Selma, Alabama
Dent McCulloughs, Atlanta, Georgia
Dr. and Mrs. C. E. Hix, Jr., Smiley Library CMC, Fayette, Missouri
Dr. Claude L. Smith, Newport News, Virginia
Dr. Claudia Heard, Tuskegee, Alabama
Dr. Jackie Ammelmon, Emory University, Atlanta, Georgia
Dr. Riley Eddlemon, Heritage House, St. Louis, Missouri
Dr. Rolla P. Andrae, The Daniel Boone House, Defiance, Missouri
Elizabeth Laughlin, Kirksville, Missouri
Georgia Historical Society, Athens, Georgia
Georgia Historical Society, Atlanta, Georgia

Hazel Luna, Nashville, Tennessee
Kathleen Wilham, Genealogical Research Publishing
Marion County Courthouse, Hannibal, Missouri
Missouri Historical Society, Columbia, Missouri
Missouri Historical Society, St. Louis, Missouri
Douglas Clave Purcell, Eufaula, Alabama
Erin D. Stephenson, Zanesville, Ohio
Robert A. Oslin, Sr., Atlanta, Georgia
Robert L. Hawkins, The Missouri Partisan, Jefferson
  City, Missouri
Mrs. Bennie Fickland, Charlotte, North Carolina
Mrs. Cecil Jackson, Selma, Alabama
Marie Pisselhorst, Palmyra, Missouri
Sondra V. Blunk, Brunswick, Missouri
Sybil McRay, Gainesville, Georgia
Angela Barnett, Eufaula, Alabama
National Archives, Washington, D.C.
Rev. Neil A. Gately, Shelbyville, Missouri
Shelby County Courthouse, Shelbyville, Missouri
St. Louis City Directory Search, St. Louis, Missouri
T. Turner, Demopolis, Alabama
Tennessee Historical Society, Nashville, Tennessee
The General Sterling Price Museum, Keyetesville,
  Missouri
Tim Burgess, White House, Tennessee
Vicksburg National Parks, Vicksburg, Mississippi
Wilkes County Courthouse, Washington, Georgia

Resources

Bennett, W. W. *The Great Revival in the Southern Armies.* Harrisonburg, Va.: Sprinkle Publishing, 1989.

Brownlee, R. S. *Gray Ghosts of the Confederacy.* Baton Rouge: Louisana State University Press, 1958.

Church Street United Methodist Church. Selma, Alabama.

Dewelly Cemetery. Kirksville, Missouri.

Dryden, Ruth T. *The Boundless Bounds Family.* San Diego, Calif.: Ruth T. Dryden, 1989.

———. *History of Monroe and Shelby Counties, Missouri.*

Forest, McDonough. *Five Tragic Hours: The Battle of Franklin.* Franklin, Tenn.: The Carter House, n.d.

Gottschalk, Phil. *In Deadly Earnest: The Missouri Brigade.* Columbia, Mo.: Missouri River Press, 1991.

Haynes, B. F. *Tempest Tossed on Methodist Seas.* Nashville, Tenn.: Methodist Episcopal Church South, n.d.

Hunting College. Montgomery, Alabama.

Irvin, Willis, Jr. *The Prayer Warrior.* Augusta, Ga.: self-published, 1983.

Jones, D.D., J. W. *Christ in the Camps.* Atlanta, Ga.: The Martin & Hoyt Co., 1887.

Merchant, J. A. *Methodism in Brunswick, Missouri.* Brunswick, Mo.: self-published, n.d.

Missouri Conferences 1860–1865. Methodist Episcopal

South. Kansas City, Mo.: Burd & Fletcher Publishers, 1907.

Pemberton Historical Park Information. Salisbury, Maryland.

Pitts, Charles L. *Chaplains in Gray*. Nashville, Tenn.: Broadman Press, 1957.

Service Records Missouri Troops. National Archives. Washington, D.C.

Southern Reader, Vol. 1, No. 1. Summer 1989. Paris, Tenn.: Guild Bindery Press.

Tennessee Conference 1865. Methodist Episcopal South.

Tennessee State Library Archives. Nashville, Tennessee. *Confederate Collection*.

United Methodist Archives. Nashville, Tennessee.

Vicksburg National Military Park. Vicksburg, Mississippi.

Warren, M. B. *The Hills of Wilkes County, Georgia*.

Williams, Walter. *History of North East Missouri*.

Books by E. M. Bounds

We have tried to list all available editions. We apologize to any publisher for books that may have been inadvertently omitted.

The Best of E. M. Bounds. Grand Rapids, Mich.: Baker Book House, 1986.

Catching a Glimpse of Heaven. Springdale, Pa.: Whitaker House, 1985.

The Complete Works of E. M. Bounds on Prayer, eight books included. Grand Rapids, Mich.: Baker Book House, 1990.

E. M. Bounds on Prayer. Springdale, Pa.: Whitaker House, 1997.

The Essentials of Prayer. Grand Rapids, Mich.: Baker Book House, 1991; Springdale, Pa.: Whitaker House, 1994.

Memos to God: A Prayer Journal and Organizer With the Writings of E. M. Bounds. Chicago: Moody Press, 1994.

The Necessity of Prayer. Springdale, Pa.: Whitaker House, 1984; Grand Rapids, Mich.: Baker Book House, 1992.

Obtaining Answers to Prayer. Springdale, Pa.: Whitaker House, 1984.

Possibilities of Prayer. Grand Rapids, Mich.: Baker Book House, 1992; Springdale, Pa.: Whitaker House, 1994.

Power Through Prayer. Springdale, Pa.: Whitaker House, 1983; Chicago: Moody Press, 1985; Grand Rapids, Mich.: Baker Book House, 1992.

Power Through Prayer and Purpose in Prayer, combined edition. Uhrichsville, Ohio: Barbour & Company, 1989.

Powerful and Prayerful Pulpits: Forty Days of Readings. Darrel D. King, ed. Grand Rapids, Mich.: Baker Book House, 1993.

Prayer and Praying Men. Grand Rapids, Mich.: Baker Book House, 1992.

Prayer and Revival. Darrel D. King, ed. Grand Rapids, Mich.: Baker Book House, 1993.

Purpose in Prayer. Grand Rapids, Mich.: Baker Book House, 1992; Springdale, Pa.: Whitaker House, 1997.

Reality of Prayer. Grand Rapids, Mich.: Baker Book House, 1992.

Treasury of Prayer. Leonard Ravenhill, compiler. Minneapolis: Bethany House Publishers, 1981.

Weapon of Prayer. Grand Rapids, Mich.: Baker Book House, 1991; Springdale, Pa.: Whitaker House, 1996.

Winning the Invisible War. Springdale, Pa.: Whitaker House, 1984.